*The Literary Enterprise in Eighteenth-Century France*

*Le Parnasse français.*
Engraving after a bronze by Louis Garnier, 1718.
From Evrard Titon Du Tillet,
*Description du Parnasse français* (Paris, 1727).

# The Literary Enterprise in Eighteenth-Century France

by Rémy G. Saisselin

UNIVERSITY OF ROCHESTER

Wayne State University Press

Detroit, 1979

Library of Congress Cataloging in Publication Data

Saisselin, Rémy Gilbert, 1925–
  The literary enterprise in eighteenth-century
France.

  Bibliography: p.
  Includes index.
    1.  French literature—18th century—History and
criticism.  2.  Litterateurs—France.
3.  Criticism—France—History.  4.  France—
Intellectual life—History—18th century.  I.  Title.
PQ261.S26      840'.9'005      78-11253
ISBN 0-8143-1618-2

Frontispiece by permission of the Bibliothèque nationale, Service photographique.

# Contents

## Author's Note

At the request of the publisher I have translated all French passages, prose as well as verse. In translating verse I have not attempted rhyme, and I have aimed to give the spirit of the text rather than the letter. Certain French expressions and titles have been left untranslated if there are no satisfactory English equivalents.

Many of the works I discuss were published in more than one edition. Textual citations, unless otherwise indicated, are to the specific editions listed in the Bibliography.

# Introduction

## The Writer and His Image under Louis XIV

Taking the term *literary space* as a metaphor for the writer's experience of literature, I shall, in this work, be concerned with the consciousness men of letters came to have of themselves, their métier, and literary history in the course of the eighteenth century in France. I have not sought to be exhaustive; I do not wish to be exhausting, and the reader is most kindly asked to read this book, not as a dissertation in the tradition of present French microhistory, but as a modest essay concerned with this question: what was literature to some of the writers of the Old Régime?

I have borrowed the term *literary space* from Maurice Blanchot, for whom it seems at times to signify the writer's experience of being nowhere, adrift in some infinite space coextensive with the endless flow of language. But the eighteenth-century writer had a different sense of orientation because he did not, like Blanchot and other contemporary French critics and poets, discuss the act of writing on the metacritical level made possible by the meditations of critics, poets, and philosophers after Mallarmé's famous throw of the dice. If, for the writer as perceived by followers or admirers of Blanchot, writ-

7

ing is an activity without end, interminable and incessant, in an alienating space created by an alienating act, by contrast the eighteenth-century writer found himself in a space with rather well-defined contours, crossroads, signals, and directions, with familiar places, institutions, and objects. Blanchot's writer is in an inner space which is infinite, for this space is his inwardness combined with the extension of language. It is also a space associated with death, and therefore I tend to think of it as a dark Pascalian space. But the eighteenth-century writer moved in a landscape, like Gil Blas or Rousseau on his way to and from Paris or Dr. Johnson on his way to London. If I start this book with an image of a writer on a road on his way to a city, it is because it seems to me that the study of literature has become so analytical, metacritical, and psychoanalytical that modern academics and critics have constructed a literary history, or at least an approach to literature, as abstract as Heinrich Wöllflin's art history of pure visibility. The logical conclusion of such an abstract and analytical approach is Blanchot's meditation on the act of writing, the book as a species of metacritical object, and the end of literature.

After the nineteenth century's literary history of lives, influences, movements, or ideas, we have now a literary history of pure thought, pure form, and the pure act of writing, or what one might call a literary history of inwardness, of the unconscious, and of the tricks of language, all divorced from history. Racine is abstracted from his historical milieu, and the practitioners of this abstract approach prefer writers like Mallarmé, Kafka, Proust, Artaud, Valéry, Musil, or Flaubert. Thus while the field of inquiry becomes more and more rigorous in critical terms, requiring a knowledge of philosophical terms and an acquaintance with metaphysical approaches, the area of literary study tends to become more and more narrow. A great many writers find themselves eliminated from consideration by an approach which tends to concentrate on writers hyperconscious of the problems posed by language, the act of writing, the gratuity of art, and their ironic position in a world in which the value of literature is in doubt. But this approach also makes for disregarding the existence of literary institutions, history, and even that object we pick up without paying too much heed to it, the book.

It may be that the development towards greater and greater abstraction and the concentration upon a few, highly selected writers mirrors a late phase of the bourgeois view of literature. Just as bourgeois literary history implied a linear view of its development, a Whig interpretation of literary history as accomplishment, and the establishing of literary values, with literature in effect coming to represent the capital of a culture, so one may speculate that the abstract, inward, analytical, and self-doubting approach to literature and writing reflects the bourgeoisie's own doubts. At the same time the refined, restrictive, and analytical approach has been seconded in its tendencies by the democratization of the teaching of literature, which necessitates its professionalization and the construction of programs of courses as against the old joys of musing, discovery, and speculation. This has also contributed to a narrow view of literature and its history. Journalists, hacks, amateurs, printers and publishers, book dealers and collectors, and institutions such as libraries, academies, literary salons, and cafés, the milieu of letters, have all but disappeared from our literary histories. The great names survive in the curriculum, and periodically new writers are added to the established fund of literary values, just as *poètes maudits,* dadaists, surrealists, and antinovelists are added to reading lists. But what obtains in effect is still the type of history of literature which arose in the nineteenth century, a history separate from books, separate from publishing, separate from the writer's perception of himself and his métier. It is the professor's view of literary history.

This established, linear history documents a kind of upward mobility in the sense it may be made to begin in the Middle Ages and proceed to the twentieth-century classroom. It is thought of mostly in terms of texts which can be fitted into the ultimate ideal anthology, containing a beginning, middle, and end, and commented on in the present. For some time now, however, thanks to French historiography, there have been attempts to supplement this type of literary history with a broader approach. Chapters on the conditions of literary life, the social background of writers, and the world of publishing are added to existing literary histories. A good deal of research has been conducted on the book trade and publication in the eighteenth century, and we have thereby come to know how much typographers were paid in Yverdon, their rate of absenteeism, Rousseau's laundry bills, and the profits of under-the-cloak booksellers. The substratum of literary history currently seems to absorb more and more attention as we come to know more and more about the formerly disestablished literary history. This research, conducted sometimes by teams under the direction of a research director, will continue to uncover more facts, and we will come to know so much that the individual mind, bewitched by the mass of empirical data, may be stunned into total paralysis.

It is not my intention to discount or doubt the value of such research, but it seems desirable to offer a counterview of this empirical literary history of the Old Régime by creating a synthesis based on the image of the Temple of Fame, a device often used in the eighteenth century to set up hierarchies of literary and artistic values. The metaphor of literary space also seemed a useful tool with which to order some of the empirical data. Claude Cristin's unfinished dissertation, *Aux origines de l'histoire littéraire,* published after his death by his friends in 1973, may serve as the starting point for any work in this area. It promised a novel approach to the study of literary history and the inception of a literary consciousness. Cristin suggested beginning with images of literary men and early varieties of literary history. The image of the Temple of Fame further suggested an aim for writers, for it was an imaginary location in that metaphoric literary space, as well as a hierarchy of values, and thereby offered an alternative to linear history. But the metaphor of space, as I discovered, soon suggested other areas and other itineraries.

Today images of social types—statesmen, politicians, film stars, sports heroes, criminals or noncriminals, successful writers (by which we mean rich ones)—are created by the vast machinery of the media. In the seventeenth century the image of the writer was of his own fabrication, and according to Cristin may be found in two general sources: in belles lettres, in genres such as comedy, satire, dedications; and in those works in which writers were concerned with books, libraries, and literary reputations, the world of learning and of the book. A study of the man of letters as such, in seventeenth-century France, was notable only by its absence. When one did appear it was translated from the Italian of Father Daniello Bartoli's *Dell' huomo di lettere* of 1645. Other views of the man of letters were scattered and fragmentary, though it is possible to construct two opposed pictures of how the man of letters saw himself and was perceived by those aware of his existence. Cristin distinguishes between negative and positive images. The first type appears in the minor modes of literature, such as poetry, satire, and novels, where writers are represented as pedants, penniless poets, college regents, learned doctors, or scholars. There is a fine picture of the negative type in Boileau's first satire.

> Damon, that famous author whose fertile muse
> So long amused both court and town,
> But who, of rough and prickly wool attired,
> Spent summers shirtless and winters coatless,
> And whose dry frame and famished mien,
> Found themselves cheated for all his fame—
> Weary of wasting at rhyme his efforts and fortune,
> Of borrowing from all and earning from none,
> In rags and flat broke, at a loss where to turn,
> His misery his only burden, today took flight. . . .

Molière's savants and poets, Vadius, Trissotin, and the Master of Philosophy of *Le Bourgeois Gentilhomme,* also come to mind, and a similar view of the despised author interrupting a dinner party of actors is given in Alain-René Lesage's *Gil Blas.*

> Our little lackey came to tell our mistress for all to hear: "Madam, a man in dirty linen, muddied up to his back, and who, if you'll pardon me, looks quite like a poet, asks to speak to you." "Have him come up," answered Arsenie. "Let us not move, gentlemen, it is an author." Indeed, it was one whose tragedy had been accepted and who was bringing my mistress a role for it. His name was Pedro de Moya. He entered with five or six deep bows to the company which neither rose nor greeted him.

Many such passages could be gathered to create images of poverty, misery, ridiculousness, vanity, social and amorous ineptitude, arrogance, miserliness, ugliness, negligence of costume and hygiene, lack of elegance, vulgar taste or none at all, gluttony, and parasitism.

The negative image of the writer, from the poet to the pedant in a college, is what could be characterized as a species of "intellectual lumpen parasitariat," especially since the poor writer was judged against the warrior and in relation to those who made up high society. Poverty, rags, and hunger are thus common traits of the self-portrait of the writer in the seventeenth century, and it is significant that society was already being blamed for his condition. Poets, it was argued, unlike doctors and judges, do not have the means to become rich quickly and cut a fine figure in the world, and princes all too often preferred the company of financiers and *nouveaux riches* to men of letters and education. This complaint must be understood within the context of a time in which luxury was coming to play a more and more important role in society. In addition, the negative view of the writer was still determined by his position in a society dominated by a feudal class contemptuous of letters and learning and a nobility at times still illiterate. This situation contrasts with that of earlier periods in France, as under Francis I or during the period of the Pléiade, as well as with the importance accorded letters in Elizabethan England or the use found for writers in the period of Addison and Swift. The writer, and especially the poet, thus appeared as a marginal figure in a difficult economic and social situation.

The solutions for the poet, as Cristin sees it, were of two sorts: he could, as Mathurin Régnier expressed it in his third satire, renounce courtly ambition and hope his patron would offer a small living in the country where he might enjoy life with some measure of security and independence. His marginality thereby accepted, the poet would retreat into poverty and take on the figure of an antique sage. This is a frequent image of the writer in the country, as witness Boileau at Auteuil, and in England, the very well-to-do Pope at Twickenham. The image need not imply poverty, but rather independence, and it can be set off against the image of the writer in the bustle and ambition of the town. Failing this solution, one could renounce literature and find another profession, making of letters merely an agreeable pastime—a not uncommon attitude which can be associated with the courtly view of literature. But Cristin's treatment of the status of the writer in the society of seventeenth-century France shows, it seems to me, a strong class orientation which might be attenuated somewhat by taking another point of view. J. W. Saunders's approach in his *Profession of English Letters* (London and Toronto, 1964) is perhaps more suggestive. Rather than thinking of class or social orders, it might be more fruitful to think of the profession of letters as not yet defined. The writer's image in this sense is negative because his profession is not yet accepted as such by society at large and is certainly anything but autonomous. Thus there are the two extremes of the courtly amateurs and the professional entertainers, and the middling position of the writer engaged by some institution useful to the state.

Allied to this negative view of the writer, an image which is often external, insisting on the physical aspect of the writer and his gauche social behavior, there is also what might be called an "interior" negative picture, which satirizes the writer's mentality. Here, however, a distinction must be drawn. This internal negative picture is mostly taken of the college pedant, of the man of letters as a savant, and as such it satirizes erudition. One may think of the Academy of Laputa visited by Captain Gulliver or of the Academy of Bordeaux proposing, as the subject of the prize essay for the year of Candide's arrival in France, why the wool of the sheep brought back from El Dorado was red. However, the satire of the savant as pedant also found expression in works such as Thémiseuil de Saint-Hyacinthe's *Le Chef d'oeuvre d'un inconnu, poème heureusement découvert et mis au jour, avec des remarques savantes et recherchées, par M. le docteur Chrisostome Mathanasius,* which first appeared in The Hague in 1714 and had eight other editions, the last appearing in 1807. This "Masterpiece of an Unknown" was prompted by controversies which arose about

Madame Dacier's translation of the *Iliad* and was intended as a satire of the pedantic supporters of the ancients in the then reigning "battle of the books."

Antoine Sabatier de Castres, literary critic and enemy of the philosophes, wrote of Saint-Hyacinthe: "If some lucky genius had heaped the same ridicule upon the philosophic mania as this author did on pedantic erudition, the philosophes would already have disappeared, like the commentators"(*Les Trois Siècles de la littérature française*, 4:22). The *Chef d'oeuvre d'un inconnu* is a work which is still readable today and is not without some contemporary relevance. It is an extended commentary and explication of a popular song of five strophes which begins:

> Colin sick in bed
> The other day,
> Of serious malady
> Thought he would die;
> Yet could not sleep
> For thoughts of love,
> And longed for his girl
> In his arms all night.

But the explication and commentary is preceded by statements of false censors, laudatory verses on Dr. Mathanasius in Hebrew, Greek, Latin, English, Dutch, and French, as well as several prefaces, odes, epistles, and remarks in honor of the great doctor, and a complete list of the works of literature he mentions in the course of his analysis, which begins with the *Amadis de Gaule* and ends with the *Traité sur l'homme en quatre propositions*. The commentary on the first strophe begins with a reference to Horace and is no less than fifty-one pages long, with references to Anacreon, La Motte, Fontenelle, Boileau, Homer, Virgil, Racine, Abbadie, Ronsard, Molinet, Rémy Belleau, Clément Marot, the Académie française, Seleucus, Alexander the Great, Antiochus, Leptine, Eristratus, Mithridates, Xiphares, La Fontaine, Chrétien de Troyes, Thibault de Mailli, Marguerite de Navarre, Mélin de Saint-Gelais, Mademoiselle de Saint-Léger, Quintus Curtius, Vaugelas, the chevalier de La Ferté, Benserade, the *Histoire critique de la république des lettres,* the *Spectator,* Mark Antony and Cleopatra, Jodelle, Dido and Aeneas, Garnier, Corneille, Portia, Madame Dacier, Madame Durand, Délie, Turnebus, Jehand Moniot, and Segrais.

The word *sick (malade)* in the first verse is commented on as follows:

> *Sick.* That is to say, *which is not well,* or as the gentlemen of the French Academy put it, *which feels some irregularity, some alteration in one's health.* And so Colin was sick, not that his health was affected by a fever or some sickness which required a doctor of medicine. He was what in familiar terms one would call *ill at ease [être tout je ne sais comment];* in the low style, *so-so [être tout chose];* and in the loose style, *in the dumps [être tout évêque d'A . . . ].*

[1:16]

The erudite Doctor Mathanasius then is reminded of similar sicknesses in history, such as that of the son of Seleucus Nicanor, one of the captains of Alexander and founder of the Seleucid kingdom, namely Antiochus, who fell madly in love with Stratonice whom his father had married in a second marriage—a love which made him as sick as Colin was for Catin. And so on, verse by verse and sometimes word by word for all five strophes, making a 264-page commentary of tautologies, irrelevant erudition, and ample quotations which show off to great advantage the vast knowledge of Dr. Mathanasius.

Needless to say, this type of negative image is rather different from the usual satirical view of the penniless poet, in that it transcends a physical and social type to portray a mentality. The implications of the satire are important because they signify a limit: one form of knowledge, erudition, *le savoir,* is in fact being held up to ridicule. This may be of consequence in the vision of the Temple of Fame in which the savants are separated off from the poets, and at the same time ridicule of misapplied erudition may have played a role in preparing for the reorganization of knowledge effected by the Enlightenment.

Cristin points out that the negative image of the writer, though fabricated by himself and the result of his social situation, was most frequently presented to readers who belonged to fashionable society. It was the image not so much of how writers saw themselves as of how the court and town saw them or reflected them. But writers, as creators of their own image, could also conceive another view; one could consider, for example, that erudition need not always be ridiculous and that not every scholar was a Mathanasius. This positive view of the writer and his profession is to be found in a different type of writing altogether, in what Cristin refers to as the *histoire littéraire des savants,* a general category which he further subdivided into two general types, bibliographies and biographies. The progress of printing made for marked increases of books and therefore of bibliographies as each nation sought to make compendia of the writings produced by its savants. These early bibliographies were sometimes called *bibliothèques* ("libraries"), and may be likened to the parallel cabinets or collections of pictures and curios in the fine arts. Similarly the biographies were historical dictionaries of the lives and works of writers, modeled on those of saints, great men, and painters. Cristin argues convincingly that these compendia do not signify a regression of intellectual activity or speculation, but rather an expansion of it, and that the bibliographies and repertories allowed the organization and comprehension of this expanded production. The word *bibliothèque* thus used appears in the sixteenth century; *bibliographie* was used in 1633 and was accepted in the *Dictionnaire de l'Académie* by 1672. These terms lead to our first well-defined view of literary space in the Old Régime, that of the Republic of Letters.

# *I*

## *The View from the Library*

*When I entered the land of letters, they were still flourishing, and several great personalities maintained their glory. I have seen letters decline and finally fall into almost total decadence; for I know almost no one today whom one could call a true scholar.*

Pierre Daniel Huet, bishop of Avranches

By the end of the seventeenth century the Republic of Letters had constituted an autonomous space which, in its metaphoric as well as literal sense, was the library: the *bibliothèque* as a bibliography or collection of books, or the library as a man-devised space constructed for a defined purpose. Associate the *bibliothèque* as bibliography to that other form of writing of the period, the biographies of writers, and one may put it that the library represented the museum of the Republic of Letters. As against the social space of town and court, as well as the marketplace, the library created the space within which writers found themselves mirrored in a positive image. This was their world, distinct and separate from the noisy world in which they were perceived only in negative terms. But the library was more than this psychological locus: it was positive in other respects because it offered various sinecures, and its role in the formation of literary history must also be taken into account.

It is in the library that one may seek the beginnings of literary history, the awakening of a consciousness of literature, the constitution of a literary world and domain. This literary history begins not as a linear form such as we have since become used to, but as bibliographies and biographies.

17

From our vantage point in historical time one could argue that these are but the building blocks of literary history rather than a form of it, but one must remember that historical thinking did not always espouse the developmental form. The library supposes a view of literary history at variance with that subject as taught in universities in our own time. In the late seventeenth century one viewed literature less in terms of its history than as a fund, an acquired body of books and manuscripts, and the first task of the literary historians was not to delineate a development but to classify materials. This fact implies a very broad view of literature, making it coextensive with the world of books, old and new, their authors, printers, critics, and the libraries in which they could be found—thus including subjects which in our day have been separated out of the realm of letters referred to as literature. Cristin notes that the *Nouvelle Bibliothèque des auteurs ecclésiastiques* of 1693 is a bibliography arranged by content as one would order a library, and so it also effectively serves as a guide to a library. "The structure, the very materiality of the books, takes on the value of an image. And one realizes that the representation of themselves writers offer each other encloses them, in a manner at once figurative and concrete, in their own universe" (p. 45). While this remark evokes a closed space, the library was not a limited space in a figurative sense, because the reader's imagination and the book allowed access to other times and other places. The writer was free because his imagination was free, because so many books were so many ways out of the prison of the negative image.

"Letters" was understood to include all activities of the mind from poetry through the sciences (meaning bodies of knowledge) and theology, a broad view which obtained well into the eighteenth century. Literature in its modern sense was a late arrival, according to Cristin.

> It is necessary to remember that literature, as we use that word today, did not exist before 1750. By isolating certain particular works from the whole printed production of former times, the modern notion of literature has created a false concept of an

autonomous realm of creators whose poetry, theatre, and novel would have been the entire domain.

[P. 89]

Such a domain was indeed distinguished within the broad area of literature as *belles lettres,* humane letters as distinct from sacred literature, or else the term referred to poetry and eloquence and the knowledge of poets and orators. But in no case did it mean the practice of poetry or any other genre; rather, it signified the knowledge of a particular area of letters. Yet by 1740 belles lettres was coming to be associated with the practice of poetry, eloquence, and history. This trend is not unconnected to the debate between the rationalists (of the Cartesian persuasion) and philosophes on the one hand and their more literarily inclined adversaries on the other. In the early eighteenth century, then, literary history was a complex structure coextensive with the Republic of Letters. One indication of this complexity lies in the various contemporary schemes for classifying books, a subject Cristin covers in detail. A close look at one representative "literary history" may serve to illustrate both the complexities involved when literature is made coextensive with the world of the book, and the assumptions underlying the approach that makes literature coextensive with the world of the book.

### Adrien Baillet and Literary Judgment

Adrien Baillet is one of those writers who would probably be excluded from modern literary history and transferred instead to a separate history of scholarship, bibliography, or perhaps criticism. He represented all these specialties, as well as being a historian, a biographer, and a hagiographer. He was born 13 June 1649 at La Neuville, near Beauvais, of very poor parents, and was educated in a nearby convent of the Cordeliers. From there he was sent on to study at the Collège de Beauvais where he became teacher of the humanities, took holy orders in 1676, was parish priest for a short time, and finally was appointed librarian to Chrétien François de Lamoignon, attorney general and président à mortier of the Parlement de Paris, a man of great learning whose preceptor had been Father Rapin. Baillet, as Louis Moréri's *Le Grand Dictionnaire historique* reports, spent the rest of his life in Lamoignon's service "without mixing in the affairs of the world" to die young on 21 January 1706.

Baillet represents one very comfortable solution to the problem of being a man of letters in a society dominated by feudal values and money, for there were ways of leaving the world without leaving town. One was to find a living in the church; another was to become a librarian, and the role of the latter in the formation of literary history cannot be overestimated. The early works of literary histories were intimately linked to the existence of libraries. Baillet's view of letters is a case in point, for it is the outcome of his work as Lamoignon's librarian. To be sure he had always worked a great deal and distinguished himself by his knowledge, but the splendid library now given to his care provided the sources for his vast *Jugements des savants sur les principaux ouvrages des auteurs,* which first appeared in 1685 and remained unfinished at his death. This work can serve as an admirable introduction to the Republic of Letters as then constituted, for it is a bibliography not only of books, but of authors and opinions about books and writers, and thus represents literary history as an acquired fund of books, knowledge, and opinion. The wide range of literature as then conceived may be measured by the table of contents, a classification of types of writers and books.

A complete outline would be very long, but an analysis of Baillet's six major divisions will suffice to indicate the breadth and comprehensiveness of his views of literature. The first division lists printers, critics, and all other writers concerned with the establishment of texts, language, and books. The second division is among the most varied and the most difficult to summarize. Briefly, it deals with those called poets, from versifiers to writers of treatises on poetry, but also includes all those writing about the vast world of the fantastic or imaginary—the world of superstitions, festivities, myths, divinities, apparitions, and dreams. The third of his major divisions is given over to the discussion of historians, chronologists, and biographers, while the next concerns writers on the sciences and the arts, from naturalists to writers on fortifications, architecture, and lives of artists. The last two major divisions cover civil, ecclesiastic, natural, and moral law and theology, religion, and the writings of the church fathers and scholastics.

For modern readers this is a most unusual literary history, for we are used to thinking of history in different terms. Not only is Baillet's method inspired by the library, but it also makes no distinction between professional writers and those who have simply written one or more books. And there is more to consider, for this mass of work, this concept of literature as coextensive with the world of learning, also supposes something else: this vast body of knowledge is not regarded as objective, but as inseparable from opinion. If our literary historiography supposes writers and history, Baillet's view from the library also supposes readers, and the body of his work is preceded by a consideration of human opinion in regard to books. In the twentieth century his prefatory essay might be described as a phenomenology of reading or of criticism, for it is nothing less than an examination of the relation between the writer and his book and the book and the reader, and encompasses the variety of prejudices that operate as readers read and form opinions about books and authors. It is of considerable interest partly because it outlines the beginnings of criticism's consciousness of itself as a special activity, but even more because of what it reveals about literary life within the Republic of Letters and the space of the library. While the library is a secure position from which one gains a positive view of the man of letters and a sense of the obvious worth of literature, yet the life of letters does not appear to be characterized by peaceful study, intellectual pleasure, and impartial judgment. The view from the library is not, in short, a view of the garden of Epicurus. One perceives rather the consequences and risks of liberty. The image is the inner dimension of that picturesque if negative exterior image of the man of letters sketched in the satirical literature of the time. But the inward negativity is far more complex than the outward view held up to the public. Sartre wrote that man is condemned to be free; in Baillet it is the author's book that is condemned to exist in a free space. In his considerations of reading and criticism, writers and publishing, Baillet discourses on the meaning and implications of involvement with letters. These opening pages are his *What Is Literature?*

To enter the Republic of Letters is to enter a republic of liberty; indeed, writes Baillet, as there are no civil laws to forbid anyone to be an author, so there are none to prevent anyone from being the censor or judge of persons who wish to appear in public as writers. This liberty is the very essence of literary space, an open field in which the writer is on his own, in which he might be plundered and fight back, but history shows no example that this liberty may be repressed. Neither Richelieu nor the Académie française was able to prevent private and public judgments of plays being represented on stage, and readers enjoy and use their liberty without regard to their capacities for good judgment. Few are indifferent enough not to wish to state their opinion of an author. The public loves to criticize, which is not as unjust as those who argue that this taste for criticism is a sign of man's corrupt nature would have it. Once an author has appeared in print he must look upon the work as no longer his, considering it with the same indifference which the reader has for the person of the author. The only limits to critical liberty are wisdom, modesty, good sense, the light of reason, and other such qualities. This liberty is quite independent of the author. He is free only to write or not to write; once the choice to write has been made, he is committed, and it is the reader who is free to judge. Baillet here makes an interesting distinction between a short-term liberty, that of the writer to choose, and that of the public, whose liberty continues from generation to generation, century to century, for as long as the memory and works of writers last.

The glory of the reader's liberty would thus seem to exist at the expense of the writer, whose condition is generally admitted to be humiliating and miserable. But the author's servitude is voluntary, for no one forces anyone to write. The public therefore must not be expected to be interested in the author's excuses for a work which it finds to be ridiculous, offensive, or foolish. A work is judged on its merits, not on the circumstances or the excuses given by an author for publishing it, nor even on his social rank. Generally the public will not heed arguments explaining why such and such a work had to be published; excuses simply will not be admitted. As a result of this general liberty of the public to judge as it pleases rather than as authors would wish, all writers are equal as regards public censorship and judgment, and all, including the greatest, have been ill treated at some time. It is up to the authors to learn something from the criticism, to learn nothing, or to rise above it.

There is a simple explanation for why everyone is subject to criticism: while few books are bad throughout, there are even fewer which are universally good. And most books are poor not so much because of their subjects as because of the form and the writing. Considering that nothing is perfect in the world of men, the best book is the one which has the fewest faults. Yet critics are not agreed as to what makes a good book. For some good sense suffices, while others look for four characteristics: discernment, solidity, order, and brevity. Still other critics consider knowledge, exactitude, harmony, and proportion, while there are those for whom a book must above all be a vehicle containing everything necessary to improve man's mind, and these probably form the majority of critics in the Republic of Letters. On the whole, continues Baillet, the public now wants well-written works, but one must remember that what holds for the present was not always so, and that for a long time church writers disdained what they considered the vain ornaments of style.

It is important and necessary that authors be judged and censured because of man's corrupt nature. For a book is an image of man and man is sinful, that is, ignorant and filled with concupiscence, and most books are affected by these faults. In short, and Baillet quotes from Father Pierre Nicole's *Traité de la manière d'étudier chrétiennement,* man's character, sins, passions, and views all show in his work. This attitude goes some way toward explaining the eighteenth-century form of criticism called *personnalités*—that is to say, judgments from the work to the character of the author. It is also important when one considers that not a few critics graduated from ecclesiastical establishments. Furthermore, this moral-Christian approach explains both censorship on the part of the state and its complement, the doctrinally well-founded fear of the possible corrupting influence of "bad books." The danger is twofold, for the human heart is an infected vessel; there is danger from books but also from ourselves as readers of books, and it is this which explains the Index of forbidden books, compiled to protect the faithful from corruption.

In France, Baillet explains, the right to examine books in regard to their potential for harm is shared by the bishops and the doctors of theology of the Sorbonne, though there are those who contest the latter's right to this censorship, arguing that it is a matter which belongs only to priests. Be that as it may, by a decree of 1624 four doctors of the Sorbonne were appointed as censors and approbators of all new books published in the kingdom. But while the judgment of ecclesiastical works is under the jurisdiction of the church, their condemnation, suppression, and destruction is the duty of the secular power. This is the established usage, but it is a moot question whether, on the part of the authors, this obligation to be censored is active or passive. Most authors do not seek approval before publication. A Christian writer should submit his work to examination before publication, and this practice might also be useful for other writers, for a good censor may act as a master who helps to correct and perfect a work. It is obvious that Baillet is uniting two different types of censorship, doctrinal and formal, under the single term *criticism,* and other critics would share this confusion. The positive aspect of understanding criticism in this way, according to Baillet, lay in that the insistence on form had done much for the progress of the arts for over a century, though he admitted that good writing depended on the censors chosen. But all these considerations merely showed how difficult it was to judge a book well.

24

Baillet observes: "For if it is difficult to speak of one's own work without being suspected of vanity and self-deference, it is no less difficult to speak of the work of others without being accused of malice or flattery and even blindness" (1:19). If a critic is just, exact, and severe, he will draw on himself the hatred and envy of biased and ill-formed minds; if he judges ill or allows himself to be corrupted, he will be a laughingstock or object of contempt. And thus Baillet comes to the conclusion that the art of criticism is subject to more danger than any other profession in letters. In order to be a good critic, "one must possess the composite of all the excellent qualities of which a few suffice separately to make a man of competence in other areas of knowledge" (1:22).

Despite these difficulties, Baillet found it possible to outline the moral and intellectual qualities which make a good critic. The first and most important is "common sense and right judgment in discerning the true from the false" (1:22). But, as he points out, there is no quality rarer among critics and writers. Most men have a false judgment, and nothing is more difficult to correct. Unlike Descartes, Baillet thinks that common sense is not "as common a quality as one may imagine" (1:23), a remark which places him in the family of minds to which Bayle and Fontenelle also belonged. The critic also had to possess knowledge, and his understanding ought to be broader than that shown by the writer in the book he is asked to judge. However, while it was agreed knowledge is necessary to judge contents, there was no agreement concerning the type of knowledge necessary to judge style or manner. Many relied on the estimations of women and even of servants in judging an author's style, and Father Malebranche, the famous metaphysician, thought that taste, fashion, language, and style were spheres in which women were particularly good judges, though he thought they had no head for hidden truths. Certain orators and playwrights also relied on the people to judge of their style. But critics should be endowed with other inborn qualities, such as force and penetration, and moral qualities such as integrity, vigor, and severity. It was these moral qualities which maintained the liberties of the Republic of Letters, its discipline and its equality. Finally, a critic ought also to be modest and kind, for these were the qualities which won readers' hearts, established a critic's reputation, and gained the confidence of the author.

Unfortunately, the faults of critics were more numerous than their virtues. Not only did they often possess the contraries of the desirable qualities, but they were also only too often guilty of hasty judgment and pedantry, a failing many held to be inseparable from the profession of letters. But the existence of excellent critics demonstrates that pedantry is a personal and particular fault, not general to the species. Baillet goes into this failing in considerable detail, which may well indicate the extent to which his age was prone to it; it is part of the negative image of the writer, and also shows that many if not most critics were in fact savants connected with universities. He gives numerous examples of pedantry, such as picking out the bad spots of a work rather than the good; showing off one's knowledge; piling up Latin and Greek quotations to no purpose; getting excited about minor errors and the etymology of a word; taking an author to task for not sufficiently admiring Cicero; being a partisan of some ancient philosopher as if he were a member of his own family; and other such personal predilections.

Then there was chicanery, or looking for faults and quarrels in order to seek a triumph over an author, a malevolent form of pedantry closely linked to another common fault among critics, malignity. This manifested itself as a positive aversion for those judged, as envy, and as lack of sincerity. Sometimes, indeed, critics were more corrupt than the books they found to be so, and Baillet thought this trait was endemic: "This malice which is common almost to all men rules particularly among critics" (1:35). It explains denigration, lack of generosity, and seeing spots where others do not see them, just as malignity also makes one divine hidden intentions where the author had none in mind. But worst of all, it shuts a critic's eyes to good qualities.

Love and hatred also interfered in critics' judgments. These unstable passions cloud judgment. Many have been blinded by personal inclinations, though not all judgments by friends or enemies are necessarily false. But amour propre is a poor judge too; it may well be the first of human traits and certainly is the last a critic will shed, for it only passes with his own passing. In truth, thought Baillet, few are those who judge without regard to their own interests, passions, and beliefs, so that often a critique told one more about the critic than about the author he examined. Where religious communities were concerned, amour propre was simply communalized into what was then called *amour de société et de communauté,* and in the twentieth century might be called a company or departmental mentality. Baillet of course had many opportunities to see such collective pride at work since the disputes between Jansenists and Jesuits were far from suppressed in his day. The later disputes between the philosophes and their enemies were in part inspired by a similar psychological phenomenon.

But quite apart from the varieties of amour propre which interfered with right judgment, there were other factors at work which were not particular to individuals, but rather typical of classes, nations, and professions. Indeed, as one reads this amazing introduction to the *Jugements des savants,* one begins to wonder whether true judgment is possible at all. Baillet's attitude toward this question was similar to Montaigne's, and he saw that the Republic of Letters was an all too human realm. The doubt increases as one scrutinizes the long list of prejudices Baillet discusses in the second part of his introduction, for though these prejudices based on education, profession, nationality, and institutions are not all false or unreasonable, they are almost ineradicable. And good or bad, prejudices create mental blocks (or, as Baillet puts it, *bouchent l'esprit*) and impair the true judgment necessary for right reading. Either the mind is not free to receive new ideas or tends to falsify them.

Baillet observes in particular: "Among the many prejudices which affect our reading and estimation of authors, none has more weight or has been prescribed for a longer time than that in favor of the ancients" (1:41). His discussion of the Quarrel of the Ancients and the Moderns illuminates the psychological background of the scholarly world involved in the controversy. His remarks point to the importance of the quarrel in freeing the mind from prejudices and various other hindrances to new readings and new thinking. His image of a blocked mind or spirit is especially apt, for if the prejudices he describes had not been overcome (or come unstuck), the Enlightenment might not have occurred, or at least would have taken an entirely different and perhaps nonliterary form. For according to Baillet, the prejudice in favor of the ancients was a powerful passion which extended beyond books to monuments, medals, and inscriptions. It is as if the entire world of early eighteenth-century culture was a hurdle to any new intellectual departure; the prejudice was a refusal to think, since it rested on acquired, accepted, authoritative knowledge; it was a blind faith, an immovable object in the path to progressive forms of thought. One may see it in terms of an opposition between an ossified Renaissance humanism and a new form of thinking, based not only on rationalism in the manner of Descartes but also on forms of thought derived from the natural sciences.

Baillet's analysis thus turns into a phenomenology of the scholarly mind and the scholarly establishment as the uncritical conservators of knowledge or opinions. Indeed, one may say that, according to Baillet, the partisans of the ancients were not really interested in truth, but only in antiquarian knowledge. "For do not imagine that those who grow old bent over the books of Aristotle and Plato can always make good use of their liberty of mind. For they ordinarily use so much time reading these books only to try to enter into the spirit of their authors, and their principal aim is to know the real opinions they held, rather than those which ought to be held" (1:44). Their scholarship was not impartial; Baillet saw it as an aspect of amour propre, since this type of knowledge made for an association of the ancient and glorious author with his modern commentator. The glory of the ancients was, so to say, annexed by their modern partisans.

There were still other prejudices to be considered in regard to the reputation of authors, critics, and books. The social position of a writer, his personal authority and reputation, his fame or lack of it, his religious, national, or regional traits, his personal character, and, for that matter, even his humors in the old medical sense affected critical judgments. Even the size of a book affected what was thought of it. "A book's reputation is made as soon as its size has struck our imagination, and it often passes for read when it has only been seen" (1:150). Some judge a book by its title, others by its price or its rarity, and the publishers also affect its reputation in certain cases. The size of an edition is no indication of the value of a book, for it is well known that bad books proliferate. One should consider that good books are written for the few and are hard to sell; that the populace thinks only in terms of quantity; and that the money a writer earns is no indication of his merit. In the end one must use one's own judgment to assess a book, and not accept the opinions of the world.

Baillet's reflections may strike the modern reader as wise scholarship informed by a healthy skepticism concerning human nature. His tone is equally that of a man above the fray; but he was unable to escape controversy, even though he reported not his own opinions so much as those of others in his survey of literature. Some of his contemporaries were not at all pleased to learn what others thought about their work, their friends, and their literary values or models. One of the readers most displeased by Baillet's book was the haughty, satirical, erudite Gilles Ménage, an important if irascible figure in the Republic of Letters. He undertook to write a detailed rejoinder, the *Anti-Baillet,* published in 1690 and republished in 1727 and 1730 along with a new edition of Baillet's *Jugements des savants.*

The *Anti-Baillet* is itself an interesting example of one type of book which is probably inseparable from the literary space of the library. It displays the kind of knowledge prized in that space as well as the prickly nature of its inhabitants. In his preface Ménage outlined Baillet's wrongs against himself: Baillet had called him a pedant, described his morals as pagan, called doubts upon his authorship of the *Origines de la langue française* (1650), and written that Ménage praised his own eulogies too much. This, Ménage continued, he did not mind very much because he had grown accustomed to libels written against him. But he would not accept Baillet's intrusion into the Republic of Letters.

> But I could not read without astonishment that a new arrival on Parnassus, one who had never spoken to men of letters, who knew no sciences, had not read any originals, and was but the copier of copiers, had the temerity to judge all authors in all languages and all sorts of sciences and the insolence to speak with contempt of the most famous writers of the realm.
>
> [P. xxvi]

Ménage of course counted himself among the most celebrated writers of the kingdom and decided to defend himself and his friends by doing his Christian duty toward Baillet's book.

> I can assure the reader . . . that never has a book been printed in which errors are so gross and plentiful. And this I do [that is, point out the errors] not only to defer to M. Baillet's request to his readers to inform him of his mistakes, but through Christian charity, that he may see the error of his ways, and oblige him, by showing him his lack of ability, to speak next time with respect of those to whom he owes respect.
>
> [P. xxxi]

The red pencil was to be used with the utmost politeness and in the name of Christian charity.

The result is a book in which one very learned man finds fault with another very learned man, and in which chapter headings warn the reader of Baillet's ignorance as a librarian, his ineptitude, errors, faults, mistakes, misattributions, and even lies. Ménage of course graciously corrects Baillet where necessary and loses no opportunity to show off his erudition and astounding knowledge of both ancient and modern books and authors. The affinity of this type of writing with the controversial literature of the church is clear in Ménage's scholastic recourse to authorities. But one may also think of the pedants Vadius and Trissotin ridiculed by Molière as well as the commentator of *Le Chef d'oeuvre d'un inconnu*. Indeed, perhaps more than Baillet, Ménage belonged to a generation of literary scholarship which would be questioned more and more by the end of the seventeenth century and in the early eighteenth. The type of knowledge he possessed and showed off was looked upon with skepticism by minds attuned to developments in the natural sciences, and the savants came to be ridiculed by poets and wits in the name of taste and style.

## *The View from the Library as Literary History*

The literary space of the library implies works other than the controversies between, and the satires of, pedants and savants. It made for diverse ways of writing about men of letters and literary history, and it also formed certain attitudes towards the life of letters which are no longer current. These writings and attitudes clarify the life of the Republic of Letters about 1700 and the self-definitions of men of letters as these took shape before the triumph of the philosophic party.

If Ménage's vanity was such that he lent himself readily to the negative view of the savant, this was hardly the case of Bernard de La Monnoye, who had a reputation as man of letters and gentleman which was beyond criticism or question, never subject to ridicule, and earned respect even from certain members of the aristocracy. His is a fine example of the type of fame one could gain within the space of the library without ever writing a book. His literary reputation was based solely on remarks, occasional verses, letters, academic prizes, and notes for editions written by other writers or about other writers. Above all he was praised for his modesty, disinterestedness, love of study, vast knowledge, and avoidance of cabals, so that he was made to appear a man of wisdom, a learned gentleman who knew how to avoid the trials and tribulations particular to the Republic of Letters. La Monnoye's image as a man of letters was entirely positive, and he may be regarded as one of an ideal type that existed before another was evolved to push him into the past.

J. A. Rigoley de Juvigny, who belonged to the same social-professional class as La Monnoye, brought out a three-volume edition of his works in 1769 and also wrote a life of La Monnoye as an introduction to it, the *Mémoires historiques sur la vie et les écrits de feu M. de La Monnoye, de l'Académie française* (Dijon, 1769). This life is interesting not only for

*31*

what it has to say concerning La Monnoye, but also for what it indicates about the literary values associated with the library, and, by extension, with the parlementary class, at a time when these values and forms of thought were being questioned by the creators of a new literary space, the philosophes. La Monnoye and his biographer represent the literary ideal and commitment summed up by the library, and the story of his life serves as a foil to the new literary values and mores associated with the eighteenth century and the philosophes.

Bernard de La Monnoye was born in Dijon on 25 June 1641, into a family enjoying what Rigoley de Juvigny calls an *honnête fortune*. The family's fortune was sufficient to allow him to attend the Jesuit college in Dijon, where he soon showed talent for Latin poetry and epigrams in the style of Martial; soon Greek and Italian were also familiar to him. His biographer remarks that La Monnoye was lucky to have been educated before the frivolous eighteenth century, when the models of antiquity still counted for something and one would have blushed to publish a work without solid knowledge. Later La Monnoye was sent to Orléans to study law. He stayed there several years in order to become acquainted with legal writers whose works had become rare and hard to find. It was in Orléans that he developed into a judicious and exact critic. He was received an advocate to the bar of Dijon in 1662, but did not practice law, preferring to devote himself entirely to letters. "Content to exercise a sweet and tranquil empire upon himself, and thereby enjoy a solid and cloudless happiness, he little cared to show himself upon the world's stage and sacrificed without regret the glory he could have gained by his eloquence" (La Monnoye, *Oeuvres choisies,* 1:8). He made friends in Dijon among the learned of the parlementary class known for their interest in literature, antiquarian studies, and even poetry. Rigoley de Juvigny presents La Monnoye at this stage of his life as a young man of lively temperament who knew how to overcome the passions of youth, a mastery permitted by letters; literature, as wisdom in action, purifies and elevates the soul. "When such a happy inclination carries one forward, and one is the born friend of truth, then mores are purified, the spirit enlightened, the soul lifted and expansive. Such is the fruit which study must necessarily produce" (1:13). What emerges from this biography is a positive picture of the man of letters as savant, sage, and true philosopher, a man who espouses wisdom. From the historical perspective it is clear that what is being praised is the view of literature of the parlementary class, and that the idealized portrait of La Monnoye also serves as an antiportrait. "To live within and under the protection of the law, to do good, and respect truths beyond the feeble human understanding: that is what constituted the true philosopher [in contrast to the philosophes of 1769]. The title had not yet been abused to deceive the weak, flatter the passions, and destroy virtue" (1:14).

Indeed, in contrast to the literary mores of the eighteenth century, Rigoley de Juvigny implies that La Monnoye was so modest that for ten years no one realized the depth of his knowledge; yet he had acquired the temperament and genius of an ancient. In the quiet and obscurity of his study he became a connoisseur of letters known only in the narrow circle of his friends, though eventually his fame would spread and he would be known in France and abroad as an excellent critic on whom French and foreign savants relied. He did this not by publishing, but by reading odes, discourses, and other works to acquaintances in Paris. He also wrote the *Observations sur l'anti-Baillet* which later became the *Remarques sur les Jugements des savants, d'Adrien Baillet* incorporated in editions of Baillet's work; in it La Monnoye corrected Baillet's errors, and he was praised for his precision, clarity, and vast knowledge. But La Monnoye must also have "corrected" very differently than Ménage, for Rigoley de Juvigny, using him as an example of a fine critic, defines criticism as a talent which deserves esteem only under certain circumstances. "The talent of criticism is rare and difficult. But it is estimable only insofar as it is joined to an exquisite discernment, maintained by a profound and varied erudition, exempt from ill humor and passion, and has only instruction as an end and truth and honesty as guides" (1:22). It was this talent and this wisdom which allowed La Monnoye to triumph over the contemporary condition of the man of letters, a condition which was generally ungrateful and difficult, implying hard work, long study, and long hours—all for a public which often judged writers severely and amused itself at their expense. Writing was a profession in which quarrels all too often turned into bloody wars of jealous rivals and created irreconcilable enemies. But the writer who is not jealous or envious, joining eminent knowledge to pure mores and a sweet character, truly deserves the esteem of the public, for such a man belongs to himself and also enlightens mankind.

La Monnoye's literary successes began with a competition for the Academy prize for poetry in 1672: he submitted a poem called "The Fury of Dueling Abolished by Louis XIV," which was the first of several such competition successes. He won further prizes in 1675, 1677, 1683, and 1685. He also wrote Latin poetry which was highly regarded by his contemporaries and published a collection of Burgundian carols, adapting the local patois to more urbane requirements. He also corresponded with Pierre Bayle, who held him in high esteem for the remarks he had written about his dictionary. In 1707 he was finally persuaded by his friends and correspondents to move to Paris, which facilitated his election to the Académie française in 1713. After his election his main work seems to have been a new edition of the *Ménagiana,* first published in 1693, which appeared in four volumes in 1715. It was well received by the learned; it was appreciated for his remarks, notes, identifications, and additions, all of which increased the original edition from one to four volumes, though some of his enemies wished to have the work stopped. La Monnoye submitted to the censors, deleted and added, but finally published the changes separately as the *Indice expurgatoire du Ménagiana* (1715). His old age was spent in relative poverty since he was ruined by the failure of Law's system; but the duc de Villeroy, hearing of his misfortune, gave him a modest pension which allowed him to live in relative comfort. He died in 1728 at the age of eighty-seven.

He was famous without really publishing a major opus. When the *Oeuvres choisies* appeared in 1769, there was still no complete edition of his works; Albert-Henri de Sallengre had compiled a selection published in 1716 and 1721, but this too contained but a minor part of an oeuvre which is made up of individual poems, editions of various authors, remarks, observations, introductions, and extracts from his letters. These letters reveal a lively and urbane man rather than a pedant, who expresses his view of the literary life of the times, of correspondence, gossip about scholars, knowledge of old and new books, and joy in the world of learning. He describes such well-known characters as Canon Denis of Orléans: "The greatest talker that ever was, quibbler, teller of trifles, who had his Horace, Ovid, and Petronius at his fingertips, and was ever followed by a group of young scholars from the university who amused themselves by listening to him—a great memory, in a word, but little judgment" (La Monnoye, *Oeuvres choisies,* 3:101). And as literary fashion would have it in those days, one wrote epitaphs and epigrams on persons known or famous in the Republic of Letters. La Monnoye did not fail to write an epitaph for Canon Denis.

> Death has dealt a mortal blow:
> She carried off Denis, and Orléans's dismayed,
> And no doubt for good cause,
> For to lose Denis is to lose one's tongue.            [3:103]

The criticism he was famous for also appears in his letters to friends. Thus he writes about a new edition of Anacreon just published by Anne Le Fèvre, the future Madame Dacier:

> I have not read the *Anacréon* of Mademoiselle Le Fèvre; I have been told it is a French version with notes. I don't know if she noted that there are no manuscripts of this author, which has made some critics suspicious, and [they] almost suppose it is a book written by Henri Estienne himself, who first discovered it but never said where or how. Be that as it may, Anacréon is wholly obligated to the French. Henri Estienne unearthed him and translated him into Latin verse. There is another translation by a priest from Bordeaux, Eli André; Rémi Belleau did one into French; Ronsard practically copied all of him in his *Amours;* Mademoiselle de Scudéry turned him, if I am not mistaken, into one of the heroes of her novel *Clélie,* and here is Mademoiselle Le Fèvre giving him a new dress:

> Happy Anacreon! Whence comes the marvel
> That the fair sex today gives thee such care?
> Thou who in former times loved it far less
>     Than boys and the bottle?         [3:202]

It is clear that the type of reputation La Monnoye enjoyed was inseparable from a wide and thorough knowledge of books, of what had been written and of the quality of texts, editions, and translations. The space of the library supposed a passion for knowledge and for books, but also for the men who possessed such knowledge and were famous for it. This interest in the learned gave rise to a type of protobiographical form published in the course of the seventeenth and early eighteenth centuries. La Monnoye's own *Ménagiana* is only one example. The *-ana* as a literary work thus deserves consideration as exemplary of one type of work which must be counted among the proto-literary histories flourishing in the space of the library.

The *-ana* were in part compiled by personal acquaintances or those who had heard anecdotes about the writer and were sufficiently interested to wish to know even more anecdotes, curious facts, and so on. All such items were deemed worthy of being recalled and published for posterity. Books like the *Huetana* (1723), *Ducatiana* (1738), *Ménagiana* (final edition 1715), and others which preceded them (such as the *Scaligerana*, 1666; the *Thuana*, the anecdotes and bons mots of M. de Thou, 1746; the *Perroniana* for Cardinal Du Perron, 1740; and the *Sorberiana* for M. de Sorbière, 1694) suppose a specific public which may readily be identified with the space of the library. It was a public restricted to the learned and possessors of libraries—professors, amateurs of the sciences and of letters and arts, collectors of books and manuscripts. It was small compared to the later reading public, but dispersed over several countries. It may also, in part at least, have been personally acquainted with the subject of the *-ana,* as La Monnoye was with Ménage, or at least curious about his life, friends, milieu, words, witticisms, and thoughts, moral and otherwise. What emerges from these *-ana* is the image of the man of letters within his milieu, among friends and acquaintances in the world of books and readers.

In the eighteenth century the *-ana* were superseded by a similar type of compilation, the *Esprit de . . . ,* but it was more impersonal. If the *-ana* may be compared to a collection of small drawings, sketches, rare prints, and curios, the *Esprit de . . .* is like the outline of a tableau. It is more concerned with the mind of the writer, with his writings, than with his personality and the anecdotal aspects of his career. The *Esprit de . . .* also supposes a wider reading public, one less personally interested in the author and less well defined. In effect, the appearance of the *Esprit de . . .* is a sign of the vulgarization of literature. Such books could be compiled by pillaging the subject's works; the *-ana* supposes a more personal, historical, social acquaintance with the man celebrated.

One may conceive of the *-ana* as the personal part of the writer who, given the erudite form of literature at the time, and given too a certain impersonal, highly formalized poetry, found no outlet in his writing for his self, for his personal wit, save perhaps as directed against others in satire. The *-ana* are thus a species of personal biography distinct from the lives being written at the same time, such as those of Jean-Pierre Nicéron, which were meant for posterity and intended as science. The *-ana* are the gestes of the Republic of Letters, as the epics were those of the feudal order. But this record keeping of the bons mots of savants and writers will later be generalized to include the witticisms of other members of society. Chamfort, one might argue, transformed the personal, literary *-ana* into the anecdotes which reveal the character of an entire ruling class.

Related to the *-ana* were works sometimes entitled *mémoires* or *mélanges.* A good example is Noel Argonne Vigneul-Marville's two-volume *Mélanges d'histoire et de littérature,* which appeared in Rouen in 1699 and 1700. While the *-ana* were usually compiled about one person, the *mélanges* and the *mémoires* may include anything connected with the life of letters. In contrast to later literary histories, the narrative in such works, unless it consists of memoirs by a single author about his life and his writings (such as the *Mémoires historiques et littéraires de M. l'abbé Goujet* of 1767) is not concerned with one or more lines of development of genres, but rather with events, gossip, portraits, bibliographical information, and also, in some cases, justifications for the study of literature. In Sallengre's *Mémoires de littérature* of 1716 there is a defense of the study of letters which is of some interest, if only because the author still found it necessary at this late date to make such a defense. He felt that the quarrels of pedants had given letters a poor reputation. But there was another reason. The ignorant were always asking: what is the use of studying literature? This was no rhetorical question, for among the poor a son inclined to letters was often considered useless, and the abbé Goujet, writer of a multivolume history of French literature, had to suffer persecution by his parents before they finally yielded to his passion for study. Sallengre, however, addressed himself to a broader question and public, and began by defining belles lettres as "the study of ancient profane authors, orators as well as historians and poets, and the reading of the works of critics who have worked to clarify, explain, and comment on these profane authors" (p. 212). Therein lies its very utility, for who can doubt the usefulness of knowing the history, mores, and religion of one's predecessors? People who doubt the utility of letters often think of criticism, but even this has its uses in the establishing of correct texts, accurate church history, and true knowledge of the ancient sciences, while erudition prevents hasty judgments, false opinions, and other prejudices. "Is it then nothing to correct our bad inclination to make rash judgments? Is it meaningless to learn not to accept lightly what passes into print? And is not suspension of belief the very nerve of prudence?" (p. 218). Sallengre finally arrives at the conclusion later trumpeted by the philosophes as if it were their discovery, that it is belles lettres which have revived the taste for eloquence, poetry, mathematics, philosophy, and the arts, and have swept away the barbarism and ignorance which still reigned over the minds of men in the sixteenth century. But the study of belles lettres also spreads a certain agreeableness over all the other sciences. Thus one ought not to take science or letters to task because some persons do study too much, becoming vain, asocial, disputatious, pedantic, and intolerant. Sallengre recommends the gentleman's attitude: study as a noble *délassement*. "M. de Saumaise used to say he threw ink on paper in those moments when others would throw dice or cards on the table, and he did it but as a game or a gentleman's diversion" (p. 221). In this way the study of letters is associated with a gentleman's leisure-time occupations and at the same time dissociated from the professional savant or teacher. But it was precisely for this aspect that La Monnoye was esteemed. Given such an attitude toward letters, it can be seen that the negativity attached to learning had in effect been overcome. Letters had, by way of the parlementary class as well as some of the ecclesiastical scholars, earned a species of noble status.

Books like the *-ana, mémoires,* or *mélanges* were supplemented by a perhaps rarer but related genre, the literary travel account, the analogue of Dr. Charles Burney's musical tour of Europe or the more common accounts of visits to view works of art. One such literary travel book is the excellent and informative *Histoire d'un voyage littéraire fait en 1733 en France, en Angleterre, et en Hollande,* published in 1735 by Charles-Etienne Jordan (1700-1745). Jordan was of French extraction but born in Berlin, former pastor of Potzlow and Prentzlow and then a resident of Berlin, friend of the young Frederick, curator of the Berlin Academy in 1740 and vice-president in 1744, as well as privy counselor to Frederick. He was also the author of a study on Giordano Bruno, an *Histoire de la vie et des ouvrages de M. La Croze* (1741), and a *Recueil de littérature, de philosophie, et d'histoire* (1730). His travel book is an account of visits to universities, well-known scholars and men of letters, curio cabinets, the studios of famous men, and also, which is quite important, libraries. The work gives a view of the literary space of the library in its various ramifications and allows us to perceive the more sociable aspect of the life of those who were lucky enough to be beyond Grub Street, though sometimes living in modest circumstances, and in effect making up a world of learning coextensive with the Republic of Letters. His narrative of his stay in Paris begins with a visit to Briasson the bookseller, rue Saint-Jacques, who tells him that the abbé Pernety is the author of the *Repos de Cyrus* and the marquis de

Saint-Aubin that of the *Traité de l'opinion;* he found Briasson a most amiable and polite man. On the Pont Neuf where booksellers had stalls he discovered and purchased a Pomponazzi *Immortalitate anima,* and one learns that the booksellers along the Seine already existed and were frequented by travelers as they are today—but with far better catches then than now. Thus Jordan's voyage is one of the discovery of books as well as of visits to libraries; one gleans a life of rare editions sought, of finding this or that coveted work, with much erudition and Latin quotation interspersed to make the account even more learned. The ex-pastor also visited the opera, much shocked and yet excited at what he saw and heard. But in the context of this study, the more interesting parts of his account concern his visits to men of letters and libraries.

He visited the library of Saint-Victor, very small it was true, but Scaliger had been wrong to say that it had nothing worthwhile and that Rabelais made fun of it with good reason. It had many volumes; there were several thousand which did not appear in the reading room and which had been placed in a separate room. He also was delighted to make the acquaintance of the abbé Dadou, the first librarian, and Monsieur Contet, his sublibrarian, an amiable young man very knowledgeable about books. The library of Sainte-Geneviève had a magnificent reading room, though unfortunately it was not well lighted. But Jordan reserved his great praises for the library of Saint-Germain-des-Prés. "There is not in all Paris a convent in which strangers find more pleasure than in the abbey of Saint-Germain; it is all science and good manners. A foreign visitor sees nothing which could shock him. Here the religious work hard at their studies and make of work their principal pleasure. Besides, this house contains the most knowledgeable men of France who devote all their studies to the good of church and state" (*Histoire d'un voyage,* p. 78). The Royal Library he considered as holding the first rank in Europe, especially for manuscripts, and it deserved being seen several times, but unfortunately the librarian, the abbé Salier, was too busy.

Besides these views of the many Parisian libraries, Jordan also offers glimpses of some of the men of letters of the time, and most of these, with the exception of Voltaire, were men of learning and of science rather than poets. Thus he visited the abbé de Saint-Pierre, well known for his schemes for universal peace, whom he found lodged in the corridor du Palais Royal, not very comfortably off. He was a tall man whose face was the image of probity, a man of sweetness and humane qualities. In contrast Fontenelle was magnificently housed, very much at ease and sharing richly in the goods of fortune, and though quite old, yet still with an alert and fine eye. As for Father Nicéron, a Barnabite, he found him gracious, polite, very well versed in literature, knowing several European languages, and very busy, and it looked as if his memoirs would not be finished very soon. Jordan was alluding to Father Nicéron's *Mémoires pour servir à l'histoire des hommes illustres dans la république des lettres,* which had begun to appear in 1727. (It totaled forty-three volumes duodecimo in 1745.) He also called on the octogenarian Father Montfaucon of the Congrégation de Saint-Maur, with whom he discussed the relative merits of Seranus's and Ficino's editions of Plato. He visited M. Fourmont, an expert in oriental languages, René Antoine Ferchault de Réamur, philosopher and physicist, and the abbé Du Bos, whom he found a delightful man: "How happy I was that day! I had the honor and pleasure to meet the abbé Du Bos, author of the *Parallel of Poetry and Painting* [sic], one of the best works of this century. He receives foreign callers most politely. His conversation is beautiful; the language is ever pure, the expressions well chosen; he first seizes upon a topic and develops it with much pleasantness. He proves his erudition, but with a precision of ideas which shows the nicety of his wit" (p. 100). He also called on the celebrated Charles Rollin, author of various ancient histories translated into many languages, and on the abbé Lenglet Du Fresnoy, who spoke boldly and freely of everything. But he also called on Voltaire, describing him as "a tall, thin young man who seems consumptive, and *caeco carpitur igne* [taken by blind fire]. He works too hard for his condition. I do not bother with what scandalmongers have to say about him; envy and malice may often have their part in it. He is polite; the conversation is lively, playful, full of sallies. He knows the beauties of the ancient poets quite well" (pp. 63–64). Judging from the use he made of his time in Paris, one may conclude that Jordan was representative not only of the amateur of letters, for had he not died so young he undoubtedly would have written more, but of the citizen of the Republic of Letters. His account provides a good view of the type of men who constituted that republic, and also of what they considered literature to be. Poetry had a relatively minor place in it. Opera one visited out of curiosity and amusement, as a tourist, but paying homage to men of learning was a duty and being received by those with an international reputation an honor. In the case of Du Bos, homage was a pleasure. One also saw as much of libraries as one could, and searched for books unavailable at home. One always found what one sought, or had not thought of, with pleasure.

Jordan's approach to letters and men of letters may be characterized as that of the connoisseur, which in turn partially explains the structure of early literary history. Baillet's work demonstrates that literary history in its first stages was primarily classification, an approach to an inherited body of works associated with the space of the library. This type of literary history, though its divisions might be arranged chronologically, survived well into the eighteenth century, along with two other types which may be associated with the same literary space: the history of the lives of men and women of letters; and the history of literary quarrels (which may be the origin of intellectual history). Abbé Claude Pierre Goujet's *Bibliothèque française; ou, Histoire de la littérature française,* which appeared in eighteen volumes between 1740 and 1756, is an excellent example of the first category, literary history which is essentially classification. The subtitle is long but revealing: "In which we show the utility which may be drawn from the books published in French since the invention of printing, as regards knowledge of belles lettres, or history, sciences, and the arts; and wherein is given the judgment of critics upon the principal works of each genre written in the same language." This his-

*42*

tory incorporates Baillet's approach, but is restricted to France and the period since the introduction of printing. Goujet's work was by no means the first such history in Europe or in France, and he had in fact collaborated on Dom Antoine Rivet's monumental *Histoire littéraire de la France,* which had begun to appear in 1733. Rivet's book was interrupted by his death in 1749 at the time he was ready to work on the twelfth-century renaissance of French letters (Cristin, pp. 96–97). His history was a grand undertaking, intended above all to be a work of reference and consultation, but it is clear from Father Goujet's introduction to his own *Bibliothèque française* that he had something else in mind and another type of reader in view. He begins by posing the question of whether French literature is sufficiently developed to introduce someone not versed in Greek or Latin to all the arts and sciences. The answer is not given, argues Goujet, by counting books produced, comparing nations, or making parallels, but by demonstrating the richness of French literature as it is presently constituted. He calls his book a *Bibliothèque française* because he deals only with French books, gives their titles and times and places of publication wherever possible, and classifies them by subject matter. In effect this scheme becomes the organizing principle of his book, which he nevertheless calls a history: "1) because by following as much as I could the chronological order of the works in each genre which have appeared in our language, I show the progress which has been accomplished in the arts and sciences; [and] 2) because far from giving a bone-dry catalogue of titles which could be found elsewhere, I stop at each work which deserves some consideration to discuss it and examine good and useful qualities; I indicate at least the principal faults which the best critics have reproved" (1:v-vi). While admitting that Charles Sorel preceded him in this task, he intends to be more wide-ranging and give complete coverage of available books. But since he does not consider himself a great scholar in the Republic of Letters, he will follow Baillet's method of reporting the critical judgments of other scholars. He does not give the lives of authors, but rather of books—what occasioned them, what disputes arose through

*43*

them, and what criticism they drew. He cites journals, literary memoirs, and the books themselves as his sources, insisting that however arduous and long his task, he wrote of no book he had not examined himself.

Goujet had a definite public in mind: those who had but a slight tincture of Latin and Greek and thus had to rely on the vulgar tongue; and those who knew no learned languages and yet had the taste and capacity for study. He specifically included women in his public, arguing that they are not the least favored as concerns the talents of the mind. He blames educational institutions for their lack of attention to women's education. And answering the critics who say that women read only frivolous works to amuse themselves, he opines that this is due to the way they are educated and brought up. In effect Goujet is saying that women would be delighted to be introduced to other types of reading in order thereby to win equality with men, "over whom they are so often superior in delicacy of wit and nicety of taste" (p. xxiii). Finally, to write such an history will also honor one's country, for a literature is the monument of a nation's achievement.

Goujet is obviously a partisan of the moderns, not only in that his enterprise proclaims the validity of French literature as a third culture vis-à-vis Greek and Latin, but also because he believes that certain genres have been perfected since their creation by the ancients. He thinks the centuries of Augustus and Louis XIV were about equal as to quality, that new genres have been created since the ancients, and that French tragedy is equal if not superior to Latin tragic poetry. "To be rich it is not necessary to possess all treasures oneself; and I think we ought to have enough self-esteem not to yield to the ancients a glory we may share with them in many areas, and which we have carried farther than many others. I believe even that the more we consider ourselves to be their emulators, the more noble efforts we will make to surpass them" (p. xxxiii). He rejects the idea of a degeneration of nature, and by extension of genius, since the ancients. If nature really had degenerated since antiquity, how could one explain the renaissance of letters in the fifteenth and sixteenth centuries? Yet he says he does not follow

Charles Perrault's modernism and sense of superiority to the ancients; he respects them and their achievement and intends to include gold as well as silver in his library.

At the end of his introduction, Goujet raised a problem which shows the degree to which learning was still dominated by what Baillet had called the "prejudice in favor of the antique." If this history of French literature proved successful, would it not discourage the teaching and learning of Greek and Latin? He answers that education ought to be geared to an individual's talents rather than being imposed upon all uniformly. Besides, it comes down to a question of inclination and the purposes of education.

> Education does not create talents; it only develops them. Whence follow two consequences: first, it is practically a waste of time to spend the precious years of youth occupied with matters foreign to the principal occupations which will dominate the rest of one's life; so that on the contrary one would do well to prepare oneself for what must always be done. Second, if talents differ, it would be reasonable to expect education to vary in consequence.
>
> [P. xl]

He argues for a modern education in the vulgar tongue, a practice which did not preclude a student's learning Latin later if he wished. Latin would survive in any event and have to be learned to fill certain posts in society. Goujet's history of French literature thus not only defined the field but also established it as a national fund or treasure. Vernacular literature necessarily found itself the rival of the still strongly influential heritage of classical antiquity.

If French literature had to define itself in relation to prestigious ancient literatures, and later to other national literatures, the history of men of letters had to contend with the negative image of the man of letters and alternative social types. A fine example of biographical literary history is Father Jean-Pierre Nicéron's *Mémoires pour servir à l'histoire des hommes illustres dans la république des lettres, avec un catalogue raisonné de leurs ouvrages,* which began to be published in Paris by Briasson in 1727. This work is international in scope, and in his preface Nicéron explains that his aim is to save many men of

*45*

letters from undeserved oblivion. Some survive because they find panegyrists, which is often the case for those who happened to be members of academies; there are lives scattered here and there in journals and books. But a compendium which would gather all these together remains a necessary task. The Germans, he writes, have been more careful than other nations in recording the lives of their savants, but they have gone too far. There is not one city or society in Germany which does not have volumes of such lives. The Italians are dry as dust and only record books. The English do best, for there is hardly a distinguished scholar who does not have his written life, an abridgement of his works, and a bibliography, but to follow this method would lead to infinity. His aim is thus to "give each author as much space as necessary to make him sufficiently known, and give some idea of his works" (p. iv). He found his sources in various authors, journals, libraries, and personal knowledge; at the end of each article he explained that he would cite some of the books he consulted, though he could hardly be expected to cite them all, for that would make the work too long. His account of the life and work of Albert Henri de Sallengre exemplifies his method.

Nicéron begins with an account of the origins of Sallengre's family and of his education, which included studies in Leyden, history under Perizonius, philosophy with Bernard, and law under Voet and Noodt. After his studies Sallengre returned to The Hague to live with his parents and to be admitted as advocate to the court of Holland. He traveled to France after the Peace of Utrecht and remained some time in Paris, where, according to Nicéron, he visited libraries and called on scholars to profit from their knowledge, even though he had reached the age when youth usually enjoys only pleasure. This contrast between the dissipations of the average youth and the inclination or even passion for study of the man of letters is not infrequent in accounts of the citizens of the Republic of Letters. In 1717 Sallengre made a second trip to France; two years later he visited England and became a member of the Royal Society. In 1723 he called on Lord Whitworth, ambassador to the Congress of Cambrai, and his brother-in-law, and also toured Gelderland. Smallpox raged there, and was fatal to his family and himself, for Sallengre died from it on 27 July 1723.

This biographical outline is then followed by a psychological portrait: "His mind was broad, delicate, ornate with much knowledge; he spoke easily but modestly of what he knew, and his conversation was as agreeable as it was useful for those with whom he communicated. His manners were easy and polished; he loved pleasure but never gave himself up to it, and his inclination always led him back to the Muses" (1:125). Nicéron also names the important posts Sallengre occupied—counselor to the princess of Nassau in 1716 and commissioner of finances of the Estates General in 1717. He then gives a list of Sallengre's writings: he collaborated on the *Journal littéraire de la Haye;* wrote a letter on the length of sermons; an *Eloge de l'Yvresse* (The Hague, 1714, duodecimo); the *Histoire de Pierre de Montmaur, professeur royal en langue Grecque dans l'Université de Paris* (The Hague, 1715, 2 vols. in 12); and a collection of satires and other occasional pieces about a famous parasite. Then there were the *Mémoires de littérature* (The Hague, 1716–1717), a short-lived journal; a *Commentaire sur les épitres d'Ovide par M. de Méziriac, avec plusieurs ouvrages du même auteur, dont quelques-uns paraissent pour la première fois* (The Hague, 1716, 2 vols. in 8); *Poésies de M. de La Monnoye de l'Académie française* (The Hague, 1716, 12 vols.); and a *Novus thesaurus antiquitatum* (1716, 3 folio vols.). He was working on a history of the United Provinces when he died. His eulogy is to be found in the *Journal de littérature* (vol. 12), written by Cartier de Saint-Philippe.

Nicéron's work, it need hardly be said, is an invaluable source for literary history and the life of the Republic of Letters. It is filled not only with bibliographical information but also with excellent literary portraits and information concerning the great variety of types and works which made up the worlds of letters and science. It is not literary history as it has come to be written since Jean-François La Harpe and the nineteenth century, nor is it criticism such as Sainte-Beuve wrote in his *Literary Portraits,* though it has some kinship with these methods, as

47

it certainly also has with later French literary studies of the "man and his works" type. But Nicéron's *Mémoirs* nevertheless constitutes a literary history made possible, like that of Father Goujet which it complements, by the literary space of the library. It is literary history conceived as the history of men of learning and of wits and poets, though these latter categories are relatively underrepresented. But literature also includes writers on the arts, such as Roger de Piles, and architects who have written on their art, such as Claude-Louis Daviler. Literary history thus exists as portraits of the writers, as a collection of little monographs as yet unconnected by any organizing principle. This kind of history makes for a picturesque view of the Republic of Letters. As in the -*ana,* the writers are not lost in abstractions; they are concretely present as individuals characterized socially, literarily, mentally, and sometimes physically. The library is also a portrait gallery.

But if so, it is the portrait gallery of men and women who, given the liberty of the Republic of Letters and the prickly nature of some of its citizens, were often given to prolonged disputes within the literary space of the library. Thus, in addition to literary history as classification and literary history as biography, there soon arose a third type, which concentrated specifically on the literary quarrels of the world of letters.

Three such works deserve mention: the abbé Irailh's *Querelles littéraires; ou, Mémoires pour servir à l'histoire des révolutions de la république des lettres, depuis Homère jusqu'à nos jours* (Paris, 1761); a book attributed to Aublet de Maubuy, *Histoire des troubles et démêlés littéraires depuis leur origine jusqu'à nos jours inclusivement* (Amsterdam, 1779), which was similar to Irailh's book but not entirely plagiarized; and, preceding both of these, an archetypal history of ideas, the *Mémoires secrets de la république des lettres; ou, Le Théâtre de la vérité* (Amsterdam, 1737). In his preface Abbé Irailh mentions another such work which he called the *Chronique scandaleuse des savants* of the abbé d'Artigny, but Sabatier de Castres implies that Irailh drew upon the *Nouveaux Mémoires d'histoire, de critique, et de littérature* of Abbé Gachet d'Artigny, which appeared in seven volumes between 1749 and 1756, and the catalogue of the Bibliothèque nationale seems to bear him out.

Irailh explains that his book is not meant as a satire of writers, but that his intention is moral: he would have writers learn to respect each other and use the gifts nature gave them to better advantage, rather than allowing themselves to be the playthings of the public. This is significant. Irailh was writing at a time when the concept or the perception of the man of letters in society had become more positive. He meant not only to show the ridiculousness of literary quarrels but also their utility; for truth sometimes emerges from these conflicts, thanks to the proofs and authorities adduced and called upon in the course of argument. He thus chooses only those disputes which he thinks significant, while deploring the fact that such quarrels should still occur in an enlightened age such as the eighteenth century. But they are part of the career of letters, and young persons entering upon such a career would do well to recall the verses of Monsieur de Fontenelle:

> In the arena you wish to enter
> First do calculate your chances:
> For you must with equal courage
> Offer your head to laurels
> And your nose to blows.

But the important point about Irailh's work is that it permits one to follow the thread of the progress of taste, knowledge, and the human mind. He divided literary disputes into three general types: private quarrels; general disputes on grand subjects of a philosophical nature; and quarrels between different religious orders or institutions. "One may compare private quarrels to single combat; general disputes to formal wars among nations; and quarrels between different institutions [*corps*] to those fights in which one calls for seconds and party fights party" (p. xvi). Examples of these different types are the various disputes between Boileau and many of his contemporaries, or between Voltaire and Desfontaines and later Fréron; the philosophical disputes between Cartesians and anti-Cartesians; and the long fight between Jesuits and Jansenists.

That this type of approach borders on what twentieth-century scholars would call the history of ideas is evident from the second and third kinds of disputes Irailh mentions, and also from the *Histoire des troubles,* in which there is a long discussion of the Cartesian mechanism (*système des automates*) concerning the souls of animals as well as chapters on disagreements in poetics. The last volume of this work also may be described as a protosociology of the writer: there is a long list, stretching from antiquity to the present, of writers jailed, assassinated, or accused of various crimes, of writers generally poor and miserable and obliged to work for a living, or even condemned to the flames.

The *Mémoires secrets* of the marquis d'Argens, on the other hand, promise more than they deliver. In the first volume the intention seems to be a debunking of the world of learning by a man who poses as a new type of man of letters, one who is urbane, worldly, and skeptical, making fun of the erudite scholar in his dust-covered study. The preface offers a negative view of the savant as bilious, vain, cantankerous, contentious, choleric, melancholic, vindictive, and presumptuous. D'Argens writes as if the Republic of Letters were a powerful establishment and he wished to cause scandal. Certainly he shows neither fear of nor respect for the world of learning, and a modern reader is reminded of recent quarrels between the Sorbonne and the so-called new critics in Paris. He sets forth his criticism in a series of propositions illustrated by historical and biographical examples: opinions are so varied, the ideas of the erudite so much in contradiction, that there can be no doubt their books are filled with errors. Scholars are prejudiced in favor of their own ideas and women are no more jealous of their beauty than men of letters of their opinions. At heart they all aspire to dictatorship on Parnassus; they are given to praise themselves, praising others only to be flattered in return, so that eulogies are but common merchandise in the Republic of Letters. D'Argens sounds like Baillet with an even more negative tone. But after this provocative preface the *Mémoires secrets* turns into a history of ideas with a strong skeptical bias, and it is possible to see in this work an aspect of the Enlightenment which is not always given its due in accounts of the eighteenth century. D'Argens represents an Enlightenment closer in spirit to seventeenth-century skepticism than to the pretensions of the philosophes.

The works of Goujet, Nicéron, and Irailh remained sources and models for later eighteenth-century literary histories produced at the very time the philosophes triumphed in the world of letters. Their continuing influence is evident in the production of vulgarizations such as Dom Louis Mayeul Chaudon's *Bibliothèque d'un homme de goût; ou, Avis sur le choix des meilleurs livres écrits en notre langue sur tous les genres de science et de littérature* (Avignon, 1772), which was soon augmented into a *Nouvelle Bibliothèque d'un homme de goût* in 1777 by none other than the enterprising and compiling Abbé Joseph de La Porte. Sabatier de Castres's *Les Trois Siècles de la littérature française; ou, Tableau de l'esprit de nos écrivains* (1773) also derives from the literary historiography of the space of the library. Sabatier de Castres combines the biographical with the critical aspects, and though he is somewhat negligent of bibliographical information, in effect he adapts these established scholarly genres to contemporary criticism. Charles Palissot also combined the biographical approach with the critical, but left out the bibliographical in his *Mémoires pour servir à l'histoire de notre littérature depuis François Ier jusqu'à nos jours* (1773). Pallisot's work, like Sabatier de Castres's, was organized as a dictionary, a structure made possible because they were in fact compiling from extant work and dealing either with authors whose lives had been written before or with living authors whose works could be criticized, even if not completely catalogued. The dictionary flourished at this time, having been made possible by the spadework of the Baillets, Nicérons, and Goujets.

Similar to these vulgarizations, but in some ways much more interesting, is Félix de Juvenel de Carlencas's *Essais sur l'histoire des belles lettres, des sciences, et des arts*, which, appearing first in 1744, may well be an ancestor of many similar works. This book includes more than biography and bibliography.

La Porte describes it in his *Nouvelle Bibliothèque d'un homme de goût* as "an abridged history of the human spirit." The description is just, since the author treats of the origin, development, and theoretical foundations of all the arts. The *Essais* is especially interesting as concerns the life of letters because there are chapters on journalists, libraries, printing, writing, academies, and related subjects. Other works of vulgarization of course appeared in the second half of the eighteenth century, but there is no need to discuss them here. Let it suffice to say, as Fréron perceived, that they were a sign of the triumph, fashionableness, and democratization of letters, but also of their commercialization. This vulgarization signifies that literature had passed from the limited space of the library to the vaster one of the literary marketplace.

Considered within the framework I have been developing, literary history may be said to begin with an extensive knowledge of books and the task of classification. Past and present are joined in this particular type of literary space, and there is as yet no question of assessing the significance of literature within the broader development of history or society. One may even consider this view of letters as timeless; books are, so to say, removed from the events and passions of historical time. Within the library they exist in a continuum peculiarly their own, as vehicles of thought, depositories of the various opinions of men of diverse times and places. To enter the library is analogous to entering a religious order: it is to leave the world. And yet this is not a renunciation, but merely, for the reader and person considering these books, musing among them, using them, a momentary removal from the fray to rise above it. Baillet's vantage point is one of detachment, that of the lettered man who lives within the moral sphere of the church. There is something otherworldly about his attitude to and views of life and letters, and leaving a parish for a library must have made little difference save that in the library one would have more books than a parish priest could ever afford. One is reminded of a reverse situation, that of Ernest Renan leaving the seminary of Saint-Sulpice for a species of lay clericature, outside the church yet continuing the virtues he had been taught in the seminary: poverty, modesty, politeness, and austere mores. Of course Baillet and other savants of his day did not have to leave the church to pursue the truth or to be scholars. But another writer also comes to mind—Julien Benda and his theory of the *clerc*. Benda, upon learning he had lost his fortune, nevertheless went on living just as he had before, studying, thinking, and writing. The center of gravity of these men is study, books, thought, and right judgment, far more than it is literary glory or success, and it is in this sense that their way of life is an alternate clericature. It need not imply a monkish existence, as witness, for example, Dr. Johnson and his circle. Johnson loved the city; he was a man whose concept of literature was as broad as the view gained from the library.

While this view of letters persisted well into the eighteenth century, it was being challenged. Montesquieu, with his erudition, detachment, and his particular attitudes to writing and study, belongs to this type of literary space, as does the abbé Du Bos, Lenglet Du Fresnoy, and the abbé Bordelon, as well as numerous teachers and professors and future critics of literature working in journals. But it may nevertheless be the case that Baillet's view represented, by the eighteenth century, a summing up of the world of books, and that the Temple of Fame, despite its metaphor drawn from antiquity, was but one step in the bypassing of this world of books, learning, and a broad construction of literature. Between the view from the library and the idea of literary history as development in time stood an obstacle, the metaphor of the Temple of Taste as another principle for ordering literary production and values.

# 2

## The Temple of Fame

*Men of letters, especially poets, are like peacocks who are thrown a few miserly grains in their cages and are occasionally let out so we may see their feathers fan out, while roosters, hens, ducks, and turkeys walk about freely in the farmyard, filling their maws at their ease.*

Chamfort

Alexander Pope's *Temple of Fame* is a baroque palace; Voltaire's *Temple du goût* is more likely to make one think of a Louis XV trianon; but both are visions which define a literary space. In contrast to the space of the library, the Temple of Fame poses a distant aim, object, and hope. While the library supposed something of an ecclesiastical aura, the temple, despite its name, is secular in inspiration. The spur is fame, not knowledge, though as Pope would have it, not any fame will do: "Oh, grant an honest Fame, or grant me none!" While its space is outside the library, it is not yet the space of the literary marketplace. Indeed, the Temple of Fame or of Taste, and I shall here use the two interchangeably, poses an exclusive critical principle which considerably reduces the boundaries of literature. If the view from the library was all-inclusive as concerns the materials of literary history, the temple, set atop a steep mountain, is difficult of access and thereby exclusive. It may be considered as the product of the poet's revolt within the Republic of Letters, his attempt to establish an aristocracy of letters dedicated to Apollo and the Muses. The critic is no longer a librarian, aloof, impartial, or detached, but he is much closer to what we consider a literary critic to be, one who judges on matters of style. Like the librarian, he classifies, but according to different principles and within a far more restricted circle. The principle of the temple is also one of classification, but authors are placed in a hierarchy of perfection rather than ordered in terms of the materials of human knowledge and opinions. How this exclusion and reclassification is done may be gleaned in various eighteenth-century works from Voltaire through Louis-Sebastien Mercier and Bricaire de La Dixmérie, and while one could discuss some of these visions of the temple in detail, Voltaire's seems both best and archetypal.

Voltaire called his *Temple du goût,* published in 1732, a "bagatelle," a society amusement of mixed prose and verse. Nevertheless, this trifle made him even more enemies than he already had because it was also a piece of literary criticism. It shows the extent to which, in some circles at least, literature was being refined to belles lettres, and how taste acted as an agent of literary refinement and the redefinition of literature. The piece is an account of Voltaire's voyage with Cardinal de Polignac, the author of a famous refutation of Lucretius, to the Temple of Taste. The man of letters has left the silence of the library and the study and is now going through the world to reach a point beyond it, the point of perfection.

The road is strewn with obstacles, and significantly the first ones are the savants who occupied a prominent and very honorable place within the library's literary space. Voltaire mentions Baldus, Scoppius, Lexicocrassus, and Scriblerius—references to two real scholars and two satirical characters, to which might have been added another butt of the period, Dr. Mathanasius. Voltaire also names some near contemporaries:

> There I perceived the Daciers and Saumaise,
> Abristle all over with erudite trifles,
> Of yellowed complexion, red-eyed and dry,
> Their backs bent over by heaps of old Greeks;
> They were blackened by ink and capped by dust.
> I called out to them as we passed:
> "Are you not off to the Temple of Taste
> To wash away your dust and ink?"
> "We, sir? By heaven, what for?
> That is not where our studies be.

For Taste is nothing, and we are wont
To write out at length what was thought,
But we, sir, ourselves do not think."

Quite clearly this is the negative image of the writer slanted against one type of author in particular. Baillet did not think very differently from Voltaire, but savants were not excluded from the library. Here they are merely obstacles to taste and as such are left by the road. It is the pedant or scholar who is being excluded from literature as it is about to be redefined.

But savants were not the only obstacles to be overcome. There was also false taste, the work of the *nouveaux riches* and those who served them, the taste for Italian music, and critics such as Desfontaines, one of Voltaire's personal and literary enemies. But eventually the travelers reached the temple and found an edifice whose history corresponded to the vision of history of the classical poet: its foundations had been set in ancient Greece; it had been destroyed by the barbarians, rebuilt in the Renaissance, and maintained by Louis XIV and Colbert. The result was a classical temple distinguished by its simplicity and perfection.

The temple was surrounded by a crowd of virtuosi, artists, and judges of all sorts trying to enter, but Criticism, who kept the keys to the temple, ceaselessly repulsed the Goths seeking to break down the door. Again what is excluded is *le monde,* not in the ecclesiastical sense this time, but in the sense of *la mondanité,* the party-givers, the talentless, the hangers-on of the world of letters. Seeing Voltaire's guides approach, these flee, only to be replaced by an army of men of letters also trying to enter and begging Criticism to let them pass. It is at this point that the vision of the temple becomes a critical device by distinguishing between those who are allowed to enter and those who are made to wait. It is also here that Voltaire made enemies by upsetting established literary values through his choice. Thus Antoine Houdar de La Motte, J. B. Rousseau, Charles Perrault, and Jean Chapelain were all kept waiting, and others within the temple were described as still polishing their works, cutting out poor verses, eliminating repetitions, correcting imperfections, and even consigning entire works to the flames. Corneille burned his plays *Pulchérie, Agésilas,* and *Suréna;* Racine pondered the portraits of his heroes from Bajazet to Hippolytus, who seemed too much like French courtiers; La Fontaine excluded some of his fables and shortened almost all his tales; and even the great poet and critic Boileau was perceived to erase some unseccessful verses from his ode on the fall of Namur. Long-established literary values were dealt with severely. Rabelais was cut down to half a quarto; Clement Marot, an early Renaissance poet, was left with but eight or ten sheets; and Bayle had been abridged to a single volume, while Molière was unhappy he had been forced to write low comedy for the people and deplored some of the poor endings of his plays. But it is precisely because of these traits that these men were great: they recognized their faults and those errors from which no man is exempt.

The visit ends with a lesson. Voltaire learns that if the God of Taste is hard to please, in return he loves fully and the works he criticizes in detail are the ones he loves most. He also warns the travelers against False Taste.

> Overburdened with ornamentation,
> The voice and countenance composed,
> His graces affected and language precious,
> He takes my name and my standard.
> But the impostor soon is unmasked:
> For he is but the son of art,
> While I am nature's offspring.

Voltaire may have called his *Temple du goût* a bagatelle, but his contemporaries did not take it lightly, and it may be argued he never lived it down for as long as there were critics like Desfontaines to recall it. For the critics' view of Voltaire, including that of the great Fréron himself, was perhaps fixed by that bagatelle. The poem was immediately parodied, and Charles Jordan in his literary travels wrote of the public reaction to it: "His *Temple of Taste* has done him harm. The public cries out and thunders against this piece which speaks with liberty of certain works, reduces Bayle's *Dictionary* to one tome, and makes but little of Voiture. The Italian comedians have even played it publicly on the stage" (*Histoire d'un voyage,* p. 64).

The parody he alluded to was written by two actors named Romagnesi and Niveaux. Voltaire is made to appear on stage in the guise of False Taste; he is foppish, conceited, vain, and ridiculous, judging of all heedlessly, and finding only his own works to be good. The true God of Taste tells Voltaire-False Taste that he was charitable indeed to reduce an entire library to a brochure, and then proceeds to give him a lesson in taste. Voltaire is made to sing:

> For imagine I do know it all:
> Music, dance and architecture,
> Algebra, painting and sculpture,
> All in my brain I resolve.
> No, there is nothing I can't possibly do:
> Lyrical, dramatical or epical,
> In verse or prose,
> In Hebrew, Greek or Latin,
> History, fable and politics;
> Physics, let's add, and metaphysics.
>
> [*Le Temple du goust*, p. 42]

It is an image which would remain with him for the rest of his career: the writer who dabbles in all genres and sciences. Voltaire had dared upset the established hierarchy of artistic and literary values, and he would not be forgiven until he triumphed late in life, achieving what his critics had perceived to be his true ambition: to become the new legislator of Parnassus.

The Temple of Fame or Taste is an image whereby one could represent a hierarchy of values created by taste and discernment; it is an image of the same order as the *School of Athens* of Raphael or the later *Apotheosis of Homer* of Ingres. It is also a variant of the *Art of Poetry* of Boileau and of the images of writers produced in the seventeenth century, the negative image being reserved for certain types and the positive for those who attain fame and immortality. One may refer to the Temple of Fame device as the *Mount Analog* of the classical imagination.

In the *Apollon Mentor; ou, Le Télémaque moderne* of Charles Palissot, the narrator of his vision of the Temple of Fame is accompanied by Apollo himself, who gives him various literary precepts as they travel. The obstacles they meet are more difficult than those in Voltaire's poem, and the most obvious is a muddy trench where thousands of authors vainly strive to lift themselves out of the mire. This is a sort of hell for dry poets and their eulogists, censors, prideful and spiteful writers, and the general rabble of the Republic of Letters. Chapelain, Pradon, and Cotin are named as being held in disdainful contempt by Boileau above them. The writers in the mire represent the passions of the Republic of Letters—envy, hatred, fear—and even while these failures lament, shriek, and clamor like the damned in hell, yet they continue to form schemes of vengeance against their betters and to hope that some day their works will get them through the obstacle.

The Temple of Fame device was used by Voltaire to make certain value judgments about writers who were for the most part of the century of Louis XIV. It can also be used to classify one's contemporaries, and thereby flatter or damn them. In the *Apollon Mentor* Voltaire is characterized as a universal genius who successfully exercises his talents in all poetic endeavors, though it is admitted he overstepped his limits by writing operas. Apollo warns the neophyte of letters to be aware of his limitations: it is better to be perfect in one art than mediocre in all. The narrator also meets other contemporary writers well beyond the barrier and high on their way toward the summit of Mount Parnassus. It is not the Temple of Taste which is located there, as in Voltaire's poem, but the Temple of Memory. These writers are Gresset, Marivaux, the younger Crébillon, Linant, Delanoue, and Delaplace, of whom only Crébillon and Marivaux are still read and worth reading today. Once the summit dedicated to Apollo is reached the neophyte perceives harmony and unity. Rivalries no longer exist, natural talents are recognized, and unlike in the world below, true reputation and merit are recognized and triumph. But something else is learned in the company of the Muses: in the past the situation for arts and letters had been better than in the present. For if in the past all conspired to aid the progress of the arts, the present is too much the victim of obscure mediocrities; there are too many writers who ought never have taken up a pen. And the public, bored with the good sense of Molière, ever seeks the new, so that even trifles pass provided they are novelties. The Muses warn the young writer of the failings of literary life in the sublunary world. It is dominated by false virtues, trifles, frivolities, nonsense, and the search for novelty and financial success—all so many false paths the budding poet must avoid. After this the young writer reads one of his most recent productions, dedicated and addressed to the king. The Muses encourage him to go on, invite him to join them eventually, and he leaves Parnassus with his heart full of hope and his head filled with thoughts of literary glory.

In this version of the Temple of Fame the positive and negative aspects of a literary career reappear, but with some variation and a new element, for the dark is made darker. Failures and libelous critics are placed in a literary hell, and the past is contrasted to the present to the advantage of the past. The present is somewhat like the gutter one must cross to reach the foot of Parnassus. The "classic" is thus put in the past and its ideal in the beyond, while the present is, for the man of letters, a time of strife, danger, temptations, and a continuous struggle for a perfection which can only be rewarded by posterity.

This view of the writer's destiny is in marked contrast to that perceived within the space of the library. Baillet's long introductory treatise on books, writers, and judgments on them has something of the aura and attitude of Ecclesiastes: since opinions vary and cancel each other, reputations fade, and all books and writers end up in a library or a bibliography, may one not conclude that all is vanity? This pessimism seems belied by Baillet's gigantic enterprise, marked by his obvious love of books and work, but there is no doubt that he remained first of all a Christian and maintained that firm distinction, common and basic to the seventeenth century, between eternity and the world. Therefore Baillet believes that one may be, nay must be, skeptical with regard to critical opinion, for that is the work of men in their state after the Fall, while the realm of truth is reserved for religion.

The metaphor of the Temple of Fame also signifies a

new attitude toward literature. Letters, especially poetry, are regarded as a calling, and already in the eighteenth century one entered into literature as one had entered into religious orders. This was not yet a general view; there were still many for whom literature was far from being a sacred vocation; but it was one extreme position among poets and can be regarded as the counterpole to the view from the library. Between these extremes there was much ground for variation. The notion of perfection, and the importance lent style and the high calling of literature as an art, as well as the importance attributed to its moral content, deeply influenced those critics who took their metaphoric position as guardians of the temple seriously.

The Temple of Fame device was also used to make comparative judgments about different ages. In Nicolas Bricaire de La Dixmérie's *Deux Ages du goût* of 1769, a similar vision occurs, but it is far more revealing than Palissot's or Voltaire's because the entire achievement of French literature and art is reviewed from atop Parnassus. This, too, is but a dream—in fact, a footnoted dream. The first part of the book comprises the vision, while the second is made up of commentaries on the various arts, artists, and writers which figure in it. However, while the poet was inspired to write as was the narrator in the *Apollon Mentor,* this dream is not taken very seriously. The author ends by admitting that whatever he saw and whatever moral one may draw from it would not change the course of literature.

> The world of letters went on as before, and the vision I publish will not have the honor of changing anything. Each writer will always esteem himself more than his contemporaries; each reader will hardly esteem anyone else but our predecessors; our age will forget part of its advantages, which will be restored by the following, which in its turn will ignore part of its own merits.
>
> [P. 127]

Here the skepticism of Baillet is turned into a recognition of the vagaries of taste on the historical level. The old controversy between ancients and moderns has been adapted to a more recent age, but it is time and taste which settle the issue of this prize-giving exercise. Bricaire de La Dixmérie is far more inclusive than Palissot in his *Apollon Mentor,* and *Les Deux Ages du goût* may indeed be regarded as a short history of or introduction to the French literature and art of his time. He includes a great many writers and artists, and the negative image of the writer found in Voltaire and Palissot is very much attenuated. Chapelain is made fun of for his *Pucelle,* but he is not depicted, as other writers were, struggling in the mire at the foot of Parnassus. Indeed the Apollo of this dream, appearing as the genius of the Arts, is an indulgent god, discerning, generous, and far from the moral critic who would condemn novels because their matter is licentious. Thus even Crébillon the younger is looked upon with favor because of the formal qualities of his novels. Unlike the *Temple du goût,* Bricaire de La Dixmérie's vision is not exclusive: literature is not restricted to the poetic genres, but also includes the works of moralists, philosophers, and historians. The Genius in the end pronounces that both the seventeenth and the eighteenth centuries are worthy of admiration and neither can claim the victory in this contest between the ages. This conclusion is not without interest, for it is undeniable that the achievement of the age of Louis XIV constituted, for the French writers of the eighteenth century, as much "a burden of the past" as the past did for their Augustan counterparts in Britain. But the Genius of the Arts uses the same argument as the moderns at the time of the Quarrel of the Ancients and Moderns—that is, nature is not exhausted.

> 'Tis in vain to your views nature exhausted seems,
> For art rejuvenates and lends her back her forces.
> Behold the swift-flying eagle darting in lofty skies,
> Forgotten are his crags and disdained the earth;
> He glides among the clouds and thunder's raging bolts
> As an imperial lord of the vast universe.
> The course of genius too shows such audacities,
> And overcomes all obstacles to fly beyond all space.
>
> [P. 125]

All of these literary temples—Voltaire's of 1732, Palissot's of 1748, and Bricaire de La Dixmérie's of 1769—were preceded, not only by Pope's *Temple of Fame,* published in 1715, but in France by a rather curious bronze monument, Evrard Titon Du Tillet's *Le Parnasse français.* It represents, in visual terms, a classification of French writers according to a hierarchy of value. Evrard Titon, according to Moréri's *Grand Dictionnaire historique* (last ed. 1759), seigneur Du Tillet, belonged to a noble family which originally came from Scotland, and which had long served the king in the areas of military supplies and finances. Titon himself was a former captain of infantry and dragoons, and later maitre d'hôtel of the dauphine and provincial commissary for war. He seems to have been interested in the patronage of the arts and conceived a monument to the glory of France, Louis XIV, and illustrious French poets and musicians. This monument was *Le Parnasse français,* cast in bronze by the sculptor Louis Garnier, who finished the work in 1718. It was then placed in the main gallery on the first story of the Royal Library. Once the monument was completed Titon published a written description of it in duodecimo in 1727, which was followed by an augmented, illustrated folio edition in 1732 that also contained an essay on poetry and music, one on the origins and progress of French poetry, music, and spectacles, a Latin poem on the *Parnasse français* by the Jesuit Father Vanière, and a long list of poets and musicians, a list which Titon kept updating in two more supplements, one in 1743 and the last in 1755, thus bringing his collection of names of poets and musicians up to date. This literary explication and description of the bronze monument was not his only scholarly venture. He also published a history of patronage and other monuments erected to great men, the *Essais sur les honneurs et sur les monuments accordés aux illustres savants, pendant la suite des siècles, où l'on donne une légère idée de l'origine et du progrès des sciences et des beaux arts* (Paris, 1734). Titon Du Tillet thereby demonstrated not only the worthiness of honoring the arts and letters but also showed his monument to be but among the last of such honors paid to men of letters and science.

The monument itself (see Frontispiece) represented a rather steep mountain on which were dispersed some laurels, palm trees, myrtle and ivy-covered oak trunks. Louis XIV, portrayed as Apollo and holding a lyre, was seated on the summit near some laurel trees, above which could be seen Pegasus taking flight. The nymph of the Seine was slightly below and to the side of the king, with one arm leaning on an urn representing the springs of Parnassus. On a terrace below Apollo were the three French Graces, Henriette de La Suze, Antoinette Des Houlières, and Madeleine de Scudéry, joined by garlands of flowers interlaced with laurel and myrtle leaves, and represented in the attitude of a majestic dance executed to the sound of Apollo's lyre. Eight famous poets and one celebrated musician of the reign of Louis XIV occupy a grand terrace skirting Parnassus; they occupy the places of the nine Muses as the true models of French poetry and music. These are Pierre Corneille, Molière, Racan, Segrais, La Fontaine, Racine, Boileau, and Lully; the latter carries a medallion which is a portrait of Quinault, his librettist, signifying they are one genius in the composition of perfect operas. All these are portraits in noble attitudes. Twenty-two genii are also dispersed over Parnassus; some of these carry medallions of poets and musicians, and other such medallions are hung on the branches of the trees. Moréri's list of the names of the poets and musicians represented by the medallions is nothing less than a survey of French poetry and music from the thirteenth-century *Roman de la rose* to his own day. It includes patrons, amateurs, French and Latin poets, women famous in poetry, and musicians, a total of 365 names.

Quite possibly this *Parnasse français* was the most elaborate Temple of Fame and description of French poetry and music of the period. It differs from the view from the library in that it is restricted to poets and musicians; it differs from the *Temple du goût* and the *Apollon Mentor* in that it is far less critical, satirical, and exclusive. But like all Temples of Fame, it stressed the importance of patronage, a point also made in Titon's other work, the *Essais sur les honneurs,* which traces patronage from antiquity to the present. But there is another item worthy of note in this monument conceived by a man of arms and of the court; he considers poets and musicians as

64

contributing to the glory of a nation and its monarch, a notion far removed from the image of the penniless poet or François de Malherbe's remark that a good poet was no more useful to the state than a man skillful in bowling.

If the Temple of Fame motif generally offered a noble and lofty view of letters and Parnassus, it could also serve as satire. It had its negative image in the mock apotheosis, such as Sainte-Hyacinthe's "Déification de l'incomparable Docteur Aristarchus Masso," or the mock-academic reception, such as the "Relation de ce qui s'est passé au sujet de la réception de l'illustre messire Christophe Mathanasius" of the abbé Desfontaines. The "Déification" was published in 1732, the same year as Voltaire's *Temple du goût.* Saint-Hyacinthe restates in the form of fantasy Baillet's and his age's skepticism about men of letters, and especially pedants. The narrator of this baroque tale views the crowd at the foot of Parnassus as a comic spectacle, a babble of tongues and a grotesque mixture of national traits, customs, and costumes: "What a cacophony, Great Heavens! what gibberish!" But this was not the most striking note; for the spectator also discerned the psychological traits beneath the exterior of these men of letters.

A distracted and contemptuous expression could be seen on the faces of almost all who formed the multitude. This was due to a presumption which quite intoxicated them. Historians, poets, orators, philologists, mathematicians, even some philosophers were subject to this. It is said literary men were especially prone to this intemperance, the principal cause being the study of languages and the abundance of ill-digested matter which is always hurtful when taken unmixed with the necessary knowledge. The same pride produced a different effect on others. Instead of turning livid, these individuals contracted a vivid color and affected a-haughty bearing, as if their bombast were but a plumpness keeping them in good health.

[*Chef d'oeuvre d'un inconnu*, 2:356–57]

The narrator also perceives a poet who may be identified as Voltaire who gets himself caned by a military officer because of his effrontery. This allusion was not lost on Voltaire, who later tried to demonstrate that Saint-Hyacinthe was not the author of the *Chef d'oeuvre d'un inconnu*. In this ascent of Parnassus Voltaire never arrives anywhere near the summit; he is left to struggle with the others at the foot of the steep mountain which some, for lack of footing, attempt to climb by crawling on all fours.

Saint-Hyacinthe's Parnassus, while a pleasant work of fancy somewhat reminiscent of Offenbach's Olympus, offers a serious alternative to Voltaire's restrictions. It is a Parnassus closer to the library than to the Temple of Taste, and it is far more than a French Parnassus. It is coextensive with a Republic of Letters which grows in production and has in the course of time so changed that Apollo refused to preside over literature. And since none of the other gods would take on this task, a committee chose the illustrious doctor Aristarchus Masso, author of the *Histoire critique de la république des lettres,* who is duly deified as the God of Literature after a complicated and comic process involving the transference of his image from earth to Parnassus, animation of it by the distilled essence of his books, and purification of it in a fire of laurel wood, a process which unfortunately causes a stifling and nearly disastrous stench.

The deification of the incomparable doctor belongs more to the literary space of the library than to that of the Temple of Fame, if only because the population of Saint-Hyacinthe's Parnassus is more inclusive than that of the Temple of Fame. But it is significant that the mockery is directed at a critic, for critics were to prove formidable obstacles to the poets' dreams of glory. The view from Parnassus may imply an exclusive view of letters, but it did not exclude critics. In most cases the criticism was exercised by Apollo, but in Saint-Hyacinthe's satire, the mask is off: Apollo will have nothing more to do with letters, and the Republic of Letters' censors are shown to be the critics and savants who write in and edit journals. The Quarrel of the Ancients and the Moderns and the ridicule heaped upon pedantic learning also implied, among many other facets of a wide-ranging intellectual debate connected with authority, that a writer's fame was no longer determined by the gods, but by critics working within the sublunary space of the Republic of Letters.

Both the library and the Temple of Fame represent possible models for a literary history; both were superseded by another form of thought. The view from the library was one of informed skepticism tempered by respect for learning and love of books, as well as of belles lettres. The Temple of Fame was the preferred vision of the poets and amateurs of letters, though it was also a device seized upon by critics. In terms of my metaphor of space, the library was an interior space from which one could survey the affairs of the Republic of Letters with the knowledge that all would end in a library. Parnassus, on the other hand, was something quite different. It was a goal, a distant point perhaps never to be reached, the high ground to conquer. The view from its summit differed considerably from the perspective from the library, because the republic in the distance below was perceived as a nightmare passed through but forgotten as one basked in the glory of belonging to a court of noble spirits. What both the library and the temple have in common is a negative regard for the literary life experienced in the plain lying between the library and Mount Parnassus. It is to this plain, the territory of the Republic of Letters, this area of liberty and strife, that we must turn, for eventually a new form of literary history would emerge from its struggles, rather than from either the quiet of the library or the rarefied air of Parnassus.

# 3

## Grub Street; or, The Realities of Literary Life

*He was therefore obliged to seek some other means of support; and, having no profession, became of necessity an author.*

Johnson, *Life of Savage*

Grub Street refers to an old London street as well as a stage of literary poverty, mores, and hack writing for sometimes unscrupulous publishers, familiar to students of English letters in general, and to readers of Johnson's *Life of Savage* in particular. In this book I use the term to refer to a French version of this low literary life. For Paris, too, had its hacks, pornographers, unprincipled publishers, police spies, cafés frequented by writers, and other phenomena associated with Bohemia before it was romanticized by Mimis dying of consumption under the picturesque roofs of Murger's Paris. Grub Street may be associated with that muddy ditch which figures as an obstacle at the foot of Parnassus, and of those called to letters, many if not most were destined never to cross it, never to leave Grub Street.

A young writer making his way to Paris to seek his fortune in letters in the early eighteenth century was, despite the positive image of the Temple of Fame or even the respect sometimes accorded the gentleman-scholar, something of a negative quantity. He was nothing because he had nothing, not even property rights over what he produced in verse or prose once it had been published—and this in a society in which the individual's status was determined by his possession of a title, office, position, property, riches. To enter into letters was thus regarded as a degradation. The writer had only

*68*

his wits to count on. But if we are to believe Rousseau, whose experience was significant, there were always a few people willing to help the novice in letters with a small push: "A young man who arrives in Paris with a passable figure, and makes known his talent, is always sure of being welcome. I was; this brought me pleasure without leading me anywhere" (*Confessions,* in *Oeuvres complètes,* p. 283).

Rousseau, thanks to Gabriel Bonnet de Mably, whom he had known in Lyon, started off rather well connected. He had introductions to Gros de Boze, secretary of the Academy of Inscriptions and Belles Lettres, who in turn introduced him to other Academicians, among whom Réaumur was instrumental in allowing Rousseau to read his musical notation scheme to the Academy of Sciences. But Rousseau was socially gauche and failed to exploit his connections, for, as he put it, "with some talent to find useful things, I never had any to put myself forward" (p. 287). While his musical system failed, he continued to work on it because he counted on it to make him famous and well off. Quillau published his book on the new musical notation, supposedly at half profits, with Rousseau paying the fee for the *privilège,* or rights, but he never got anything from the book save a review by Abbé Desfontaines in the *Observations sur les écrits modernes* of 1 February 1743. But it brought him no fortune, and Rousseau supported himself by giving music lessons according to his new system to a young lady. When that ceased he found himself on the streets of Paris, where one does not live for free. He did not much alter his style of life, however, merely his subsistence level, going to the café only every other day and to the theatre only twice a week. He ceased seeing his betterplaced acquaintances, maintaining relations only with other men of letters, among them Marivaux, Mably, Fontenelle, and Diderot, who then was not much better off than Rousseau. In short, Rousseau lived through the difficulties of the beginning writer and it looked as if he would long remain in this doubtful Bohemia. He was living even below the level of the journalists so much despised by writers, for these at least worked, wrote, and earned some money. Rousseau did nothing. He read poetry and spent what little money he had left over from better days. Father Castel then pointed to another expedient for the young man in search of success: "In Paris, it is through women you get somewhere" (p. 289). But it would be another eight years to Rousseau's literary success with his *Discourse* on the arts and sciences of 1751.

Voltaire started his career against the wishes of his father, but began near the top rather than the bottom of society, and poverty was never to be a burden to him. Yet his view of the life of letters is much like that of a poor young man come from the provinces to meet with the harsh realities of Grub Street, for Grub Street was also a moral state, the negative factor in literary life; and this was not remedied by money earned from one's books. Voltaire knew this life well; he had personally experienced the perils of being a writer and a man of wit in a society contemptuous of both. His letters are thus a good source for views of the career of letters. In 1738 he wrote to one Lefèvre, who would be a poet. "The career of letters, and above all that of genius, is more thorny than that of making a fortune. If you have the misfortune to be mediocre (which I do not believe), you will regret it for life; if you succeed, you will have enemies: you walk on the edge of a precipice between contempt and hatred" (*Lettres choisies,* 1:37). For this career, far from being a life of repose in the company of the Muses, as the young poet envisages it, is a continuous struggle.

The letter is a succinct account of the difficulties of a literary career. The metaphor of the Temple of Fame (his *Temple du goût* appeared the same year) takes on concrete form in a historical setting rather than on the plane of poetic fancy. Consider, he tells the would-be writer, that you have at last finished your work; you must then solicit the censor or examiner, and it would be of great help if he were of the same opinion as you or were at least a friend of your friends. If he is not, or imagines you to be a potential rival, it will be more difficult to obtain a privilège to publish than for someone to get employment in tax farming without a woman's patronage and protection. After a year of negotiation your work finally appears in print, and now it is the critics who have their day. The gazettes of France and Holland represent just as many factions whose interest it is to be satirical, and those who write for these gazettes serve the avarice and malice of a public ever avid for scandal. You may flatter writers, patrons, abbés, doctors, publishers, and booksellers, but some critic will nevertheless pounce on you to tear you to shreds, and if you answer back, and he answers you, it is merely for the greater amusement of the public which finds both parties ridiculous.

The theatre is worse, Voltaire continued, because there you must begin by pleasing the actors, who in turn suffer the barbs and ridicule heaped on them by the audience. And so the writer has to deal with an irritated judge who passes on to him the contempt which the public has for the actors. If the work is accepted and performed, one joker in the audience suffices to turn it into a failure; if it succeeds, your play will be parodied on the stage of the *Théâtre de la Foire,* that is, at some fair, or it will be turned into an Italian farce. And you may also expect the pedants to disdain you for not "following the rules." If you bring a copy of your work to a lady at court in the hope that some reward will result, she will probably give it to her maid who will use the paper to make hair-curlers, and the valets will look you up and down with utter contempt because your poverty shows. It may very well be admitted that you are not without talent or merit, but you will still have to belong to some party or faction for fear everyone will be against you. And in Paris the young writer must remember that certain salons are dominated by women and men of reputation who preside over these feminine kingdoms. Do not think that you are appreciated for your talent, for those offices which are given to men of letters are accorded to intrigue rather than talent. Some tutor, confessor, or parasite, will obtain an office you did not even dare dream of, and in some quarter presided over by a failed writer, he will make you feel small and miserable. Finally, after forty years, you will try to enter the Academy by way of a cabal, for it is everyone's secret ambition to be of this company even though all make fun of it; but that, too, is but the shadow of a triumph. And thus on every man of letters' gravestone these verses ought to be inscribed:

> Here next the fount of Hippocrene
> Lies a mortal long abused:
> To live in misery and contempt,
>     Great pains he took.

Yet writers persist, for they are led on by the hope of glory, and in a letter of September 1732, Voltaire wrote to M. de Formont: "What work and pain for this wisp of vainglory! And yet what would we do without this illusion? It is as necessary to the soul as nourishment to the body" (1:42).

But as Voltaire knew and as the image of the Temple of Fame made clear, there were other obstacles to overcome in a career in letters, and these were not only jealous colleagues, critics, and publishers. There was also the apparatus of the state, and Voltaire was perhaps aware as no other that liberty was necessary for letters to thrive. As he wrote to a *Premier commis,* or chief clerk, on 20 June 1733: "If Milton, Dryden, Pope, and Locke had not been free, England would have had neither poets nor philosophers; there is something of the Turk in wishing to ban printing, and to restrict it too much is to ban" (1:46–47). He envied English writers who enjoyed the freedom to publish what they thought and wrote, and was convinced that they were better rewarded in England than in France. He did not know the less edifying aspects of Grub Street. He compared his exile and persecution in France to the prestige and positions of Swift, Pope, Prior, Congreve, and Addison, of whom he writes in Letter 23 of his *Lettres philoso-phiques:* "In France Mr. Addison would have been a member of some academy and could have obtained, thanks to some lady's credit, a pension of twelve hundred livres, or rather he would have become involved in chicanery on the pretext that his *Cato* contained some barb directed to some officeholder's footman; in England he was secretary of state" (p. 130). While Voltaire overlooked the disadvantages of a writer tied to a political party, he was convinced of the necessity of freedom of the press and thought authority ought to act only against defamatory libels. There were bad books in all times, and they ought not to be the concern of the state. It was for the man of taste to choose, and for the man of state to allow, both good and bad.

Voltaire also advanced an economic argument to make his case for freedom of the press, one also later used by Malesherbes in favor of tolerance toward literary production at the time of the *Encyclopédie*. After all, Voltaire wrote that chief clerk in 1733, the Dutch publishers are making millions because some Frenchmen have wit; besides, even a mediocre novel serves a certain purpose. "This novel makes a living for the author who wrote it, the publisher who distributes it, the founder, the printer, the paper maker, the binder, and the ambulant bookseller, as well as the merchant of cheap wine to whom all these people bring their money" (*Lettres choisies,* 1:47). It will also amuse women for a few days; they always need something new in books as in everything else. And so this bad novel, Voltaire continued, has produced two important things: profit and pleasure. This is a remarkable passage, pointing unmistakably to the economics of writing. The writer may be perceived as the prototype of the capitalist entrepreneur, and it is probably no accident that free trade arguments, the demand for a free press, and the growing economic independence of writers were all products of the same age. To be sure, Voltaire's economic argument is at variance with the noble view of letters as expressed elsewhere in his works; the economics of literature tend to reduce it to a consumer item, and writing could thereby be associated with a vile trade. The argument that it was a noble because intellectual occupation was still to be made. But Voltaire himself wrote mostly without regard to profit, and he was willing to use any argument in favor of that liberty of thought and press he so highly prized and so ardently sought. "A man of letters must live in a free country, or accept to live the life of a timorous slave, whom other jealous slaves always denounce to their master," he wrote to his friend d'Argental in 1737 (*Lettres choisies,* 1:65).

It is his concern with liberty which makes Voltaire something more than the continuator of the values of the age of Louis XIV and also something far more than a successful

*73*

writer as businessman. Three views or attitudes are discernible in the eighteenth century toward writing, as distinct from the broader question of the significance of literature in general. The first regards writing as a disinterested, aristocratic, gentleman's occupation which might be undertaken as an amusement, as study, or with Titon Du Tillet's serious purpose of collecting the names of poets and acts of patronage. The second approaches writing as an economic enterprise and includes that ever-growing army of persons for whom writing is an employment, as well as all those Voltaire outlines as living off a bad novel. But it can also include those engaged in the vast enterprise of the *Encyclopédie,* which brings us to the third possibility. It is possible to consider writing as a vocation, something more than a private occupation, more than economics: an activity with a mission. This third attitude is important as concerns Rousseau and the philosophes, the new type produced by the eighteenth century.

For Voltaire, the philosophes must, in the end, be the true judges of literature and the creators and leaders of public opinion. One must never forget that liberty is always threatened by the fools and the ignorant. As he wrote to d'Argental from The Hague in August 1743: "I prefer the abuse of the liberty to print one's thoughts made here [in the Hague] to the slavery in which they wish to put the human mind among us [in France]. If one goes on, what will remain for us but the memory of the glory of the fine age of Louis XIV?" (*Lettres choisies,* 1:123). To Voltaire, the prestige of French literature lay not so much in the language itself as in the books written in that language: it is thought that matters, and literature was but the instrument of mind, life, one's nation, and any censorship of mind was detrimental to the vitality of a nation. But true thinkers would always be persecuted because men were afraid of leaving the beaten path, and he who tried to enlighten mankind would ever be harassed. "Write odes in honor of my lord Superbus Foppus, madrigals for his mistress; dedicate a geography book to his doorkeeper, and you will be well received; enlighten men, you will be crushed" (*Dictionnaire philosophique,* article on men of letters). But there is worse, and here one may perceive Voltaire's personal experience: the great enemy is stupidity. Though he did not write a *Duncaid* like Pope, his entire life was a fight against the goddess Dullness and the diverse forms she took in the world. "The greatest misfortune of a man of letters is perhaps not to be the object of the jealousy of one's fellow writers, the victim of a cabal, [or] to be the object of contempt of the powerful of this world; it is to be judged by fools" (ibid.). And stupidity joined to fanaticism, as well as the spirit of vengeance, could go far, and the writer had no recourse against these. A bourgeois with some official position would always find a confrère to defend him because of common interests. But the writer was alone, like a man thrown to a wild beast in the arena.

Voltaire could survey the world of letters from the quiet of the library. His letters to Madame Du Deffand are eloquent on this score. He was also a poet with visions of the Temple of Fame. But his experience of the Old Régime in particular and mankind in general was such that it made him one of the best painters of the trials and tribulations of writers, of the Grub Street in the Republic of Letters. Voltaire's was an experience common to most writers in the early stages of their careers, and if I have insisted at some length on his, it is because it allows one to perceive the various elements of this experience so clearly. That his experience was not unique is borne out by the history of literary life.

It was a cliché in the eighteenth century to praise the age of Louis XIV and hold it up as an example of munificence to those engaged in the various arts. It looked not only like the golden age of French literature, but also like the golden age of royal liberality and a privileged period in which talent was recognized and justly rewarded. It was a time, in short, far more favorable to men of letters than the eighteenth century. Those who thus praised the former century either had forgotten or meant to forget the view of the writer represented in the satirical literature of the period. Their praise was addressed to potential patrons of the age of Louis XV, and probably to the king himself, who did not particularly like writers and who therefore suffered in the view of posterity; for it is better to have writers on one's side than in opposition. M. Pelisson, in *Les Hommes de lettres au dix-huitième siècle* (Paris, 1911), thinks the praise lavished on Louis XIV was hardly justified. He calculates that the cultural budget for pensions and academies between 1664 and 1690 was about 1,767,148 livres, and that in the following century all of the academies together never cost more than 100,000 livres annually. The pensions under Louis XIV were not paid regularly; payment ceased when funds were diverted to other uses considered more important, and the treasury did not hesitate to reduce them in times of financial difficulties. Yet these pensions, then as in the eighteenth century, were sought because they were a sign of recognition, distinction, royal favor, and prestige.

Besides pensions, there were other official sources of revenues for writers who, it must not be forgotten, could hardly live off their writing alone. There were offices and secretaryships as well as some sinecures usually reserved for men of letters. Thus there were several historiographers—of the king, of the navy, of the royal buildings, and of the Menus Plaisirs, an administration concerned with festivals, ceremonies, and entertainment; there was also the historiographer of the Order of the Holy Ghost, or of the Order of Saint Louis. One could also hope to be reader to the queen, or to the duke of Orleans, or librarian to the king or to Madame Elizabeth, or ordinary secretary to some prince, such as the duke of Orleans, the Prince de Conti, Monsieur, the king's brother, or the Prince de Condé. But none of these positions paid very much; ordinary secretaries received only 400 francs, and the other posts varied between 1,800 and 2,000 livres. The sinecures paid better; the secretary of the Dragoons got 20,000 livres, the secretary to the commandant of the Carabiniers made 12,000; the secretary-general of the Swiss cantons had a good income of 30,000 francs, and the governor of the Samaritaine, a water-pumping establishment, was paid 6,000 francs. But such places were few compared to the growing army of writers scribbling in the Republic of Letters, and those who obtained such posts were part of a literary establishment. Some writers got help of a different sort from the

Crown, namely the privilege of a lodging in some royal building, but these lodgings were generally poor.

Those without the social connections necessary for this patronage had to look for other means of support, since they could not count on living by their pens. However, though writing does not now and did not then allow the author to subsist on it, as Voltaire pointed out, it nevertheless allowed others to live off the writer's product. To write is one thing, but a book is another: it is a product which is produced, bought, and sold. Thus literature was far more than writing, critical considerations, or a mental universe: it also meant the production of books and the writer could supplement the little he earned from his creative work by various forms of writing or activities connected to this literary-commercial world. Besides encompassing picturesque low life, literary mores observed from our comfortable position in another time and another literary situation, Grub Street was also commerce.

Writers might go hungry, like the poet La Louptière, the most indigent and honest of writers, who lived on a cup of coffee a day in which he dunked some bread and who, being invited to dinner by Mercier, answered, "Oh, thank you, sir, but I ate yesterday." But if writers went hungry, publishers did not. For what the hungry wrote, the not so hungry read. The writer could do other work within the *commerce de la librairie* besides writing the masterpiece which would assure him a place in the Temple of Fame. He could do copy work, clerical work, editorial work, or give lessons in sciences he hardly understood, but as Rameau's nephew showed so well in Diderot's satire, there were ways of passing the time of a lesson by seeming to be teaching, and one learns as one goes on. One could also write sermons for preachers with little literary talent; one might become a police spy, diplomatic agent, pornographer, confidence man, private informer, or gossipmonger, as was the chevalier de Mouhy for Voltaire; or one could become the terror of the theatre world by controlling a claque, as did the chevalier de La Morlière. One could borrow money and try to avoid the creditors, or one might borrow from Voltaire, who was often generous to needy men of letters. Voltaire, however, also knew when not to be too helpful, as witness the case reported by Pelisson: "A certain La Jonchère one day wrote Voltaire: 'Here, sir, is a lampoon I have written against you; if you will send me one hundred escudos, it will not appear in public' " (*Les Hommes de lettres,* p. 173). Voltaire replied that it was worth more and the writer ought to publish it. Some writers were also plagiarists, compilers, pamphleteers, thieves of the works of others, and sellers of their own works under the name of a more famous author.

Writers could also turn to journalism and become far richer than they would otherwise be. Thus Pidansat de Mairobert, in his *Espion anglais* of 29 February 1776, reporting on the reception of M. de Boisgelin, archbishop of Aix, by the Académie française, describes the abbé de La Porte as a Grub Street success.

> He seeks neither a fortune through women nor is he avid for fame. His aim is solidity, the accumulation of money. He left the Jesuits as naked as a worm, and today enjoys ten or twelve thousand livres income. . . .
>
> Did he then obtain some benefice? Not at all. He set up a book manufacturing company and uses five or six printers at a time. He writes journals, dictionaries, travel accounts, almanacs; he abridges long works and augments short ones; he has a marvelous talent for writing the same thing five or six different ways. Besides that, he lives in a miserly way, accumulates penny on penny, and lends at usurious interest. In a word, he is a secondhand dealer of literature in every sense of the word.
> [1779, 3:43–44]

This is a passage worth pondering for what it tells about the types of books which could be produced and kept writers working. The vision of the *Temple of Fame* not only implies an inspirational view of literature, but also one which will be associated with belles lettres, so that in effect a good deal of literary production was not considered literature. One may wonder how Baillet would have regarded works such as were produced by the abbé de La Porte and compilers of pocket dictionaries, such as the *Dictionnaire portatif des beaux-arts* of Lacombe, the *Dictionnaire des artistes* of the abbé de Fontenai,

78

the *Essais sur l'histoire des belles lettres et des sciences* of Juvenal de Carlencas, the *Dictionnaire des conciles,* or the *Dictionnaire des hérésies,* which were all extracted from earlier and more scholarly works and dictionaries. Such works do have a place in the librarian's view of literature, and they ought not be disregarded by the literary historian, because they probably account for the greater part of the literary production of the period, providing work for a great many obscure writers and profits for now equally obscure publishers. It is this type of production which points to the rather complicated structure of the literary world of the Old Régime and to the existence, not only of hacks or semiadventurers, but of professional writers who were not what are now thought of as creative writers because they did not write in genres now considered literature. Yet there were a great many writers who were highly regarded in the seventeenth and eighteenth centuries who were part of a respectable Grub Street. These differed from other professionals of letters only in their poverty, lack of pensions (though not invariably) or sinecures, and lack of posthumous fame. Unlike their confrères received into the Temple of Fame, they would never be immortalized in undergraduate courses and doctoral dissertations.

This type of professional writer, content to work in relative poverty though not always in obscurity, is represented by the abbé Lenglet Du Fresnoy or by Father Bougeant. In his *Mémoires pour servir à l'histoire de la vie et des ouvrages de Monsieur l'abbé Lenglet Du Fresnoy* (Paris, 1761), his biographer Jean-Bernard Michauld writes: "Love of belles lettres is ordinarily more an obstacle than a way to fortune, and the abbé Lenglet, who cultivated the Muses by taste, almost always sacrificed his ambition and his own interest" (pp. 27–28). It is an insight which says a great deal about writers content to accept the world and the Republic of Letters as they found it. Nicolas Lenglet Du Fresnoy was born in Beauvais on 5 October 1674, studied in Paris, soon showed his inclination for the sciences, and published his first work, a theological pamphlet, in 1696, when he was twenty-two. The following year he wrote a treatise on apparitions, visions, and revelations, but he did not publish it until 1751, having revised it in 1749. But in 1698 he published *L'Imitation de Jésus Christ en forme de prières,* which had four editions, and other works in French and Latin such as ecclesiastical writers produced at this time: *Novum Jesu-Christi testamentum, notis historicis et criticis illustratum* (1703), and *Diurnal romain traduit en français* (1705). Also in 1705, the abbé Lenglet Du Fresnoy was used by the Foreign Ministry as first secretary to the elector of Cologne, Joseph-Clement of Bavaria, then in Lille with his court, and he was also asked to exercise surveillance over two of the elector's ministers. When Lille fell to Prince Eugene and Marlborough, the abbé remained behind to watch over the elector's possessions, which he did by getting Prince Eugene to give him appropriate papers. In the meantime the abbé continued to supervise foreign correspondence and was instrumental in catching a captain about to betray the city of Mons to the enemy, all the while working on an extraordinary number of literary projects. His *Traité historique et dogmatique du secret inviolable de la confession* was published in 1708; another book, connected with some disputes arising from the fall of Tournai in 1709, was published there in 1711; a book on the liberties of the Gallican church was published in 1715. In 1713 appeared the first edition of a book which would not cease to grow throughout his life, the *Méthode pour étudier l'histoire, avec un catalogue des principaux historiens* (2 vol. in 12); it had a great deal of success, finally ending up in 1734 as nine volumes, augmented in 1736 by three volumes of supplement. The first edition was soon followed by a *Méthode pour étudier la géographie.* By 1718 the abbé was involved in a diplomatic plot to replace the regent with Philip V of Spain. He was asked to untangle it, which he did, provided the plotters he uncovered would not be put to death, which was agreed to. The king granted him a pension for life.

The abbé Lenglet Du Fresnoy, in short, was in a position to find another destiny had he so wished. As his biographer writes, he could have chosen to become part of the retinue of Prince Eugene, who protected him in Vienna, of Cardinal Passionei, who wished him in Rome, or even of Le Blanc, the minister of war. But he wanted above all to be independent, even in the poverty to which he was destined; he lived in a garret rather than with a wealthy sister. His biographer also records that the abbé was several times sent to the Bastille, though he does not give the reasons for it. The *Archives de la Bastille* for the reign of Louis XV (vol. 16) do, however, indicate the reason for one of these instances: he was supposed to have written a letter signed *le chevalier de Lussan* to the comptroller-general, accusing him of using funds in a way detrimental to the king, attacking the poor and the miserable, using 50,000 livres of the king's revenue for a hereditary income drawn on the postal service, diverting 9 million livres for the India Company, and indebting the king for 1,200,000 livres on ecclesiastical livings (*rentes viagères*). Lenglet Du Fresnoy was so accustomed to going to prison that he came to expect it and used to prepare for his departure in advance. After waiting for the agent to pick him up, he would greet him, and, turning to his housemaid, call for his little bag, shirts, and tobacco, and be off gaily to the Bastille. The writer of the *Troubles et démêlés littéraires* cites him as an example of the poverty-stricken and persecuted writer.

> [He] was one of the most fecund and laborious writers France has ever seen, and one of the most unfortunate. His life was but a tissue of adventures and disgraces: ill-lodged, ill-dressed, ill-nourished, he might have consoled himself if he had been left alone to write as he wished and without regard, but the censors would not allow him this liberty, the only one he sought. If it happened they crossed out some passages, he would reinsert them at the printer's, or he would dash off some satirical traits against the censor who had displeased him; and thus it is that he lived less in his house than in the Bastille, where he was sent ten or twelve times.
>
> [2:243–44]

The so-called liberals like Voltaire, Diderot, or Marmontel were not the only writers incarcerated for displeasing various persons in high places, and the philosophes were far from being the only men of letters critical of the government and therefore persecuted.

Lenglet Du Fresnoy wrote a great deal, but as the author of the *Démêlés littéraires* put it: "We have three hundred of his volumes which have made the fortune of the booksellers rather than the author" (2:244). He furnished two articles for the *Encyclopédie*, one on the "Constitution de l'Empire" and another on diplomats. He lived as he wished, despite the Bastille, despite his poverty, keeping irregular hours and not knowing how ill-dressed he was. Yet in spite of these eccentricities and difficulties, he was received with pleasure in several Parisian houses because of his vivacity and prodigious memory, and, as the literary traveler Jordan observed, he had enough of a reputation to be sought out by visitors from abroad. His death was horrible: falling asleep in front of his fireplace, he fell into the flames. He was eighty-two. One wonders whether Lenglet Du Fresnoy does not still have his representatives today in those familiar old men of the Bibliothèque nationale, who year in and year out sit in the same places, indefatigably reading, accumulating notes for one knows not what work.

He not only wrote ecclesiastical or controversial Christian literature, but also worked in profane letters. He edited Clément Marot, wrote a refutation of Spinoza, translated Thomas à Kempis's *Imitation of Christ* into French, edited the works of Régnier, wrote an interesting work on novels, *De l'usage des romans* (1735), which, being attacked by critics, he then refuted with *L'Histoire justifié contre les romans* (1735). He edited the *Roman de la rose,* also in 1735, and produced a treatise on the education of children, a history of hermetic philosophy, various historical memoirs, a life of Joan of Arc, a course on chemistry, and numerous other works. The lengthy list of his publications represents the achievement of one life devoted to letters within a literary space which touched on Grub Street by way of poverty, yet belongs on the intellectual plane to the world of Baillet, the space of the library.

While less adventurous and shorter, the literary career of Father Bougeant is similar to that of Lenglet Du Fresnoy in its characteristics and ecclesiastical background: theological studies, erudition, teaching, and difficulties with authority. Guillaume-Hyacinthe Bougeant was born in Quimper on 4

November 1690 and entered the Jesuit novitiate in Paris in 1706. After finishing his studies he was sent to Caen in 1710 to teach humanities, and later to Nevers where he taught rhetoric. After Nevers he spent the greater part of his life in the Collège Louis le grand in Paris, one of the more prestigious Jesuit colleges of the city and the nation, and it was there he also set himself to write. He collaborated on the Jesuit *Journal de Trévoux,* but also wrote several books and plays, such as *Anacréon and Sappho,* a dialogue in Greek verse (Caen, 1712), a *Recueil d'observations physiques tirées des meilleurs écrivains* (Paris, 1719), which had three editions, with an additional volume for the second and a third for the third edition, added by the Oratorian Father Grozelier. But Father Bougeant's most serious work was a much respected *Histoire des guerres et des négotiations qui précédèrent le traité de Westphalie sous le règne de Louis XIII, et le ministère du cardinal de Richelieu et du cardinal Mazarin,* based on the papers of Claude de Mesmes, ambassador to northern courts and plenipotentiary at the Treaty of Münster, which was published by Jean Mariette in 1727. As the author of the article on Bougeant in Moréri's *Grand Dictionnaire historique* writes:

> This history has been received with praise by all those with the capacity to judge it. It is possessed of penetration and discernment, nice wit, sane judgment, light touch, pure style; it is simple, elegant without affectation, natural without being low, and the graces which may adorn such a matter have not been neglected, and yet the author has not gone out of his way to seek them.

Two works concerned with religious matters followed: a refutation of a dissertation by an Oratorian on the form of the consecration of the Eucharist and then a treatise on the same subject. Bougeant published some *Réflexions sur le poème épique* in the *Journal de Trévoux* of August 1730, another article on the recitation of ancient Greek and Roman tragedies in the 15 February 1735 number of the same journal, and then another book, *Exposition de la doctrine chrétienne par demandes et par réponses* in 1741, and in the same year a *Lettre a M. l'évêque de Marseille sur la mort du R. P. Porée, de la compagnie de Jésus.* These are all serious or even grave subjects, but Father Bougeant had a different side to him altogether. The scholar was also tempted by the ironist, satirist, and poet within him, and he thus produced two books which are still worth reading. One was the *Voyage merveilleux de Prince Fan-Férédin dans la Romancie, contenant plusieurs observations historiques, géographiques, physiques, critiques, et morales* (Paris, 1735), a satire of the novelist's imagination in the form of a novel. Today it might be called an antinovel. It is especially concerned with poking fun at the fantastic and the concept of romantic love (before it was so called) found in contemporary novels. In part this is effected by taking metaphors literally, and Bougeant thereby invented the land of Romancie, where the population lives as in novels. The second was the *Amusement philosophique sur le langage des bêtes* (The Hague, 1739), a work which belongs to a long tradition of writings concerning the existence or nonexistence of souls in animals. Bougeant, well aware of the implications of the question, facetiously suggested that animals were inhabited by various types of demons. This little work created a minor scandal, and Bougeant, who had taken an anti-Cartesian stand in the controversy, was sent by his order to teach for a time in the Collège de la Flèche, Descartes's former college.

Bougeant also wrote several plays, such as *La femme docteur; ou, La Théologie en quenouilles, Le Saint déniché,* and *Les Quakres français; ou, Les Nouveaux Trembleurs,* which judging from their titles do not suggest a very serious intent. In fact, Palissot in his literary memoirs suggests they were written against his own order. But Bougeant also produced another type of writing which does not appear in bibliographies, works which he concocted for the purpose of extra pocket money. The abbé de Voisenon tells it as follows in his *Anecdotes littéraires:* "When he needed money to buy coffee, chocolate, or tobacco, he would naïvely say: 'I am going to create a monster which will get me a louis.' It was a small printed sheet announcing the meeting with an extraordinary monster seen in a very distant land, and which had never existed." He died still young on 7 January 1743. In 1744, however, another great work appeared, the second of his diplomatic histories.

This work, the *Histoire du traité de Westphalie,* was published in two quarto volumes and was considered as highly as his book concerning the preliminaries to this treaty.

Both Bougeant and Lenglet Du Fresnoy were beyond and above what is generally called Grub Street. They were not adventurers; they were not hacks; rather, they were good representatives of the Republic of Letters. They were not rich, but they were relatively secure and belonged to that class of professionals of literature studied by Daniel Roche in "Un savant et sa bibliothèque au dix-huitième siècle (Les Livres de Dortous de Mairan)." Perpetual secretary of the Academy of Sciences, member of the Academy of Béziers, Mairan was a scholar well known and highly esteemed in his day. Of good provincial ancestry and recent robe nobility, he dedicated himself to a life of letters different from that of the library only because of the greater interest he showed in the sciences. There were, as Roche points out, a great many such professionals or technicians of letters quite different from their less fortunate if more picturesque confrères of Grub Street, for these men occupied stable places. They were members of the Académie des inscriptions et belles letters or of the Académie des sciences, or they worked in the Jardin du Roi, in the Royal Library, or in the many colleges of the capital. Some were members of one of the faculties of the university, and some even had good editorial positions on one of the literary journals or gazettes. They lived off pensions or government stipends, sometimes with additional private sources of income. Mairan, for example, had a small property in the south which he eventually sold; on the whole he lived in what is called *une modeste aisance,* mostly devoted to purchasing books. For such men, writes Roche, science, letters, erudition, were professions or at least ways of life which could also turn into honorable and honored careers whereby one might become a member of one of several possible intellectual elites of the Old Régime. There were many parties in the Republic of Letters.

Another fine example of that class of professionals of letters and learning was the abbé Jean Paul Bignon, a man of wide learning and much influence in certain circles of the Republic of Letters, and generally esteemed by those who wrote about him. He was baptized in Saint-Nicolas du Chardonnet on 19 September 1662, the son of Jérome Bignon, counselor of state, advocate to the Parlement de Paris, and of Suzanne Phélypeaux de Pontchartrain. He was the grandson of another Jérome Bignon, known for his erudition and piety, and former librarian of the Royal Library. Indeed, the Bignons had possessed the office of royal librarian since Richelieu had named the first Jérome Bignon *maître de la Bibliothèque royale* in 1642. In 1685 this office was transferred to the abbé Louvois, but it returned to the Bignons in 1719, and was to remain in that family up to the Revolution.

After his studies, Jean Paul Bignon entered the Oratorian order for several years, and then decided to devote himself to further and more profound studies. He worked fourteen hours a day on theology, jurisprudence, ancient languages, criticism, and philosophy, and with this wide range of knowledge became a famous preacher. His sermons for Advent and Lent made him well known and much sought after, and brought him to the attention of the court and the king, before whom he preached to be appointed preacher to the king in 1693. He was most versatile, and once delivered four different panegyrics of Saint Louis on the same day, one to the assembled Académie française in the chapel of the Louvre, another to the Académie des inscriptions et belles lettres in the chapel of the Oratorians, which for that occasion also included the Academy of Sciences. He was also renowned and admired for his private sermons as dean of Saint-Germain l'Auxerrois, a position he occupied from 1710 to 1721. He was received in the Académie française in June of 1693, and had also been active in the Assemblies of the Clergy for the years 1693, 1694, and 1695 as deputy for the province of Paris. He was chosen to represent the interests of the clergy to the king, who found him a man worthy of reward. He was given the living of the abbey of Saint Quentin, which brought an income of 30,000 livres. In 1701 he was appointed counselor of state as chief of the bureau for ecclesiastical affairs, a post in which he showed once more a superior ability. He often presided over the academies of science and belles lettres, and it was owing to his action that these organizations were rejuvenated. He was also an amateur member of the Academy of Painting, and when the *Journal des savants* ceased after the death of President Cousin, who had been in charge of it for several years, it was again Bignon who reestablished publication in 1702.

Bignon also played an important role in acquisitions for the Royal Library, and it is worth looking at his role in some detail, for the history of this institution is an integral part of the literary enterprise and an establishment of the monarchy. Bignon was appointed chief librarian in 1719, after the death of the abbé Louvois. At the time the library was housed in two buildings in the rue Vivienne belonging to the Colbert family, but they no longer sufficed to hold the collection. Bignon therefore decided to move the library to the Hôtel de Nevers in the rue de Richelieu, also reorganizing the staff and the collection into four parts: manuscripts, printed books, titles and genealogies, and prints and plates, each of these sections being in the charge of a keeper. Other personnel were added, such as interpreters and researchers. Bignon also extended his authority over the keeper of books at the Louvre as well as the library in Fontainebleau, and he took steps to make the office he occupied hereditary in his family, assuring his succession to his nephew, a third Jérome Bignon, who was then succeded by Armand Jérome Bignon.

Bignon took the move to the rue de Richelieu as an opportunity to make an inventory of a collection which had continued to grow rapidly since Colbert's time. At the beginning of the reign of Louis XIV the collection counted some 5,000 volumes; it numbered 70,000, without counting prints and plates, at the end of the reign and it would continue to grow in the eighteenth century. The inventory lasted from 18 October 1719 through 20 December 1720. Bignon was also instrumental in obtaining manuscript collections, rare books, and historical documents, and he also showed an interest in oriental studies. Soon after he took office, 800 volumes of Chinese manuscripts entered the library, and Bignon prevailed upon the regent to have the director of the Compagnie des Indes furnish more. In

1723 several cases of Chinese works did arrive, amounting to 18,000 books in all. Two orientalists, the abbé Sevin and the abbé Fourmont, were also sent on a mission to Constantinople to inspect the library of the Grand Turk for Greek manuscripts, but being refused entry, they contented themselves with another mission, that of gathering inscriptions and medals. Sevin, however, remained in Constantinople and in two years gathered over 600 manuscripts in oriental languages for the Royal Library. The comte de Maurepas, sometime minister under Louis XV, was interested in the Royal Library, and he also was instrumental in setting up scholarships to train young men in oriental languages so that they could copy and translate Turkish, Arabic, and Persian books. Bignon got the Compagnie des Indes to send Indian books and manuscripts, and these came steadily from 1729 through 1737. In 1741 Bignon retired to his chateau of Belle Isle and died there on 14 March 1743.

Bignon, in contrast to men like Bougeant and Lenglet Du Fresnoy, belonged to a literary establishment little discussed in modern histories of literature. This establishment can be associated with specific institutions, and, in the case of Bignon, with the scholarship associated with the parlementary class as well as the Royal Library. But this same literary establishment was also connected with scholarly research among churchmen, members of various academies, and those praiseworthy institutions, the libraries. Between the low life of Grub Street and the exalted and rarefied air at the summit of Mount Parnassus, there were thus a great many intermediate levels on which the writer might find a modest place. He might perhaps be destined to obscurity, or possessed only of a love of books without the talent or drive to write, but it is obvious from the history of the Royal Library that the role of collectors of books, manuscripts, and prints cannot be left out of a consideration of literary space.

## The View from the Chancellery

There is another institution of the literary space of the Old Régime which must be considered: censorship, or the administration of justice as it concerned the writing, publishing, and distribution of books. This does not imply a view of literary history, as does the library, but it does delineate another facet of the complex literary space of the period and, like the library, it offers another vantage point on that space.

The publication, printing, and distribution of books in the Old Régime came under the jurisdiction of the chancellor, whose will was executed by the Directorship of the Book Trade. Publishing required legal approval, which generally took two well-defined forms: the *privilège,* which included a monopoly on the work published; and the simple or sealed permission, which did not include such a monopoly, but was temporary, revocable, and renewable. But in the course of the eighteenth century another type of permission was developed, the *permission tacite,* for books which the Chancellery would neither authorize nor prohibit. The right to distribute was granted, but not the right to publish. Such books were usually printed in Paris but disguised as being published in London, Amsterdam, Geneva, or even Peking, and despite the illegal nature of tacit permissions, a record of these works was carefully kept in the Chancellery.

The chancellor himself was not directly concerned with the book trade and publication; he was seconded in this task by the office of the Directorship of the Book Trade, which Malesherbes described in a letter to Voltaire as "neither an office nor a commission, but purely a mark of confidence without provisions or brevet, and wholly dependent upon [the chancellor's] will" (quoted in Pierre Grosclaude, *Malesherbes, témoin de son temps,* p. 81). The director's tasks were various and touched on all aspects of publication and book production. Indeed, one may put it that the writer and his book came into contact with that great abstraction, society, through him, and that it was here that "society" became, so to say, tangible. It was the director who designated the censors for works to be published and saw to it they did their work well; he also kept in touch with the inspectors of the book trade and the lieutenant of police charged with enforcing the decisions of the Directorship. His office authorized and supervised privilèges and permissions and also controlled the introduction of books into France from foreign nations. He was supposed to know all the printers and booksellers of Paris and the provinces and arbitrate differences between them, check on possible ruses, stratagems, and fraud in the book trade, see that the corporations of booksellers and printers observed the regulations governing their activities, see that works written and published by subscription were actually produced, supress counterfeit editions, intervene in contentions among booksellers or between them and publishers and authors, and, finally, also see to the good repute of typography. According to Pellisson, this task was not too onerous until about 1750 because book production was not great. But with the publishing of the *Encyclopédie* and increased production of other works, the director's duties became more and more difficult.

The best view of the director's task is that provided by Pierre Grosclaude's study of Malesherbes, though this may be because the other directors have not been studied as intensely and are less well known than Malesherbes, who was generally accounted a friend of the philosophic party. Certainly he was in charge of the Directorship of the Book Trade in a most interesting period, that of the publication of the *Encyclopédie* and the sharpening of the philosophical battle. He was an intelligent and scrupulous director, but he found himself caught between the two camps and between Voltaire and Fréron, for the Directorship also got involved in what the eighteenth century called *personnalités,* personal libels and personal literary attacks. The view from the Chancellery gives, at times, a rather penetrating insight into the personality of the literary type. It is a view which could be likened to that of the enlightened university administrator beset with the quarrels of persons and departments. But Malesherbes is pivotal in another sense, as a witness of the growing importance of literature in the state and the modern world. He wrote: "The empire of literature, if I may use this expression, has made immense conquests since printing was invented, and more so in the last fifty years than all the preceding ages. Today there is almost no object of thought which cannot be the material for a book" (quoted in Grosclaude, p. 672). The implications of this were far-reaching and go some way to explain his tolerant attitude, the irrepressibility of the philosophic party, the impossibility of controlling publication, and the mounting number of tacit permissions.

The view from the Chancellery differed considerably from that of the library, an atmosphere of books and peace, thought and skepticism, removed from the fracas of ambition. In the Directorship of the Book Trade the conflicts among men of letters were always at the door, and during the time Malesherbes exercised this function, the whole question of the liberty of the press was posed, implying questions concerning liberty of thought, and both literary and political criticism. Malesherbes believed in liberty of the press, but he was only too aware that writers were particularly difficult persons. "As for men of letters, I have found that whoever wishes to decide upon their self-interest had better renounce their friendship, unless he be so partial as to relinquish their esteem" (Grosclaude, p. 150). He also was aware that complete liberty was not always desirable or compatible with the French monarchy. In Britain, where the public had a far greater role in government, a free press was a necessity. But in France the king was a master who had to be obeyed. The law was simple: no book could be published without a permission and the prior approbation of a censor. "The object of all this is to prevent defamatory writings against religion, the state, or mores, or personal and defamatory libels" (Grosclaude, pp. 185–86). Books were censured in the name of public order because the state and its various powers were supposedly founded on ancient traditions and a supernatural sanction associated with truth. It seemed reasonable that works contrary to truth should be prohibited and suppressed, if only to protect weak souls who might be seduced by falsehood. But the reality here was as different as the hunger on Grub Street from the vision of Parnassus. The tacit permissions are a case in point; another was the censors chosen to read the manuscripts authors wished to publish.

The view of the *Espion anglais,* on 22 January 1777, was that censors were not chosen from the better or even the known writers; it was neither prestigious nor lucrative to be a censor, so such appointments might be given to some tutor, valet, or secretary, though in some cases men of learning were also consulted. But an author, even after having passed the censor's reading, might be incarcerated if there were complaints about his book. Mirabeau, for example, read and reread at court, nevertheless had to go to Vincennes for his *Théorie de l'impôt,* and Buffon, Marmontel, Helvétius, and Fréron were all persecuted *after* a censor passed their works. The author went to jail while the censor was at most reprimanded or dismissed. Censors were all too human, observed the *Espion anglais:* one who is secretly ambitious to be of the Academy will censor all he deems deprecatory to it and its members. Or a censor will be hard on plays or works which are critical of actors because he does not wish to lose his entrée to the theatre. And consider the censor as would-be author asked to read a rival's manuscript! Furthermore, the whole procedure was a waste of time. The best regulatory policy was thus to introduce an economic concept into publishing, a modified *laissez-faire, laissez-passer,* since the attempt to regulate meant not so much order as arbitrariness. As Malesherbes observed, not only were censors fallible, but ministries changed: "Ministries change and principles at the same time. . . . For example, there were times when it was forbidden to publish a novel, while at others one could not even write theoretically on any aspect of government or politics" (Grosclaude, p. 186). If books were not granted permissions in France, they could be published in Holland, Germany, or Switzerland, where printing costs were also lower than in France. In effect, the restrictions, legal as well as moral, exercised by the chancellery harmed the national economic interest. The view from the chancellery, given Malesherbes and the fermentation around the publishing of the *Encyclopédie,* was decidedly a view of letters in an imperfect world, but nevertheless with important literary implications.

The author, having passed the censors and seen his book in print and distributed, still had to pass another censor, one unconnected with the legal establishment but far more formidable than some obscure clerk in the service of an administration. The official censor merely asked to delete or rewrite certain passages, to change a word here and there, but this other censor would pronounce upon the author's work, mind, personality, and very self. He was that character already encountered on the visit to the Temple of Fame, the terrible Aristarchus, or Critic.

## The Critic at the Gate

La Bruyère observed that "The duty of the journalist is to say: 'There is such a book in circulation, and it was printed by Cramoisy in this type; it is well bound and printed on good paper, and costs so much'; he must even know the sign of the bookseller, but it is his folly to wish to make a critique of it." Critics were often referred to as *ces Aristarques* by writers who neither liked nor esteemed them. The name is that of Aristarchus of Samothrace, head of the library at Alexandria from 180 to 145 B.C. and considered the founder of "scientific scholarship." Tutor to the son of the king of Egypt, Ptolemy Philometus, and editor of Homer, Hesiod, Alcaeus, Anacreon, and Pindar, he also wrote volumes of commentary and treatises on literature and grammar and no fewer than nine volumes of corrections of Homer. In the words of Moréri: "He was one of the finest and most excellent critics of antiquity, but also one of the most severe, so that it was enough for him to find a verse of Homer unpleasant to declare it doubtful" (*Le Grand Dictionnaire historique*). Aristarchus is a prime example of the man of letters as perceived from the library: grammarian, scholar, textual editor, critic, tutor, and librarian, he might have been the very model for any modern scholar-critic.

Poets admitted the necessity of placing a critic at the gate of the Temple of Fame, but when they did so they must have assumed the critic would let them pass into the sanctuary and presence of the god. It was not a well-inspired assumption; they ought to have paid more heed to the characterization of Aristarchus as severe. The tone, manner, and forms of literary discussion and its manifestation in contemporary periodicals must soon have undeceived the naïve poet. Indeed, critics were heartily detested in the eighteenth century, and Diderot, in a piece on authors and critics, describes them as savages blowing poisoned darts at travelers. While he may have had the critics of the antiphilosophical party in mind, one did not have to be a philosophe to dislike critics. The general aversion must be sought on broader grounds and reasons intimately connected with the image of the Temple of Fame.

Criticism in the eighteenth century may be divided into three broad categories. First, there were scholars and teachers who produced books which may be classified as poetics or aesthetics. Charles Rollin, for example, wrote *La Manière d'enseigner et d'étudier les belles lettres par rapport à l'esprit et au coeur* (1754), a four-volume work which had many editions and was a basic text in the teaching of literature; or there were the *Principes de littérature* of Abbé Charles Batteux, Jean-François Marmontel's *Eléments de littérature* (1787), and other such works setting forth the basic principles of literary taste and value. Second, there was the occasional criticism by poets, playwrights, writers, and gentlemen-writers who made public their opinions about any work, new or old, which caught their fancy. This type often appeared as reflections, letters, prefaces, commentaries, discourses, didactic poems or epistles, or academic discourses, and may be found in the collected works of most of the writers of the period, including in the notebooks of Montesquieu, the prefaces of Voltaire, the short pieces of Diderot, the periodical literature of Marivaux, the "Discours sur le style" of Buffon, the letter on the theatre of Rousseau, and even in private correspondence. Third, but by far the most important body of criticism, was that produced by the real targets of general dislike, the journalists who commented on the contemporary production of the Republic of Letters.

As I have pointed out, poets and writers used the device of the Temple of Fame to create an alternative scale of values, and potentially an alternative literary history, to that derived from the view from the library. Scholars, compilers, erudite critics, and lexicographers were excluded from a vision founded on belles lettres. But to the discomfort of those who might have espoused such an exclusive view of literature, the opening and closing of the door to the temple was left in the hands of critics who, though they might not always have been fair or true in their judgment, took their task very seriously. The literary-critical scene thus corresponds to the skeptical view of human nature and of the foibles of men of letters implied by Baillet. The critics professed noble aims and high principles, and judged in the name of established perfection; the poets and writers whom they reviewed felt their strictures as something less than noble.

The tone of eighteenth-century literary criticism may strike modern readers, after the "close reading" espoused by the so-called New Criticism, as rather general, abstract, or sometimes even vague in its formulations. Yet there was a close reading which is similar to some present-day critical activities. Clément (Jean-Marie Bernard, to distinguish him from another critic of the same name), a professor in the Collège de Dijon, in his *Observations critiques sur la nouvelle traduction en vers français des Georgiques de Virgile, et sur les poèmes des saisons, de la déclamation et de la peinture* (Geneva, 1771), seems to have taken delight in reading poetry with a red pencil in his hand, but he was acting within the tradition of Aristarchus, and Baillet, and others who accepted certain established models as points of reference. He accepted the idea of a Temple of Taste, using the standards of antiquity and the age of Louis XIV, against the moderns. Thus he judged the translations of the abbé de Lille not only against Virgil's poetry but also against Boileau, "for one must ever turn to him, when giving examples of taste, poetry, and reason (*Observations critiques,* p. 133).

The "burden of the past" was the burden of perfection. But while critics professed to judge according to established norms, models, and taste, all too often the personalities involved turned the critical judgment into personal rivalry. Given the nerves, prickly character, and vanity of writers, and the warfare between parties at the time of the *Encyclopédie,* authors were quick to see a personal attack in every adverse criticism. Indeed, one might argue that well into the 1750s the line between what was and what was not literary criticism was far from clear. Malesherbes's observations on this subject are worth pondering, for living at the same time as Fréron and Voltaire, he could hardly avoid involvement. As he formulated his view, it is a model of good sense and good critical principles. "My principles are that, in general, literary criticism is permitted, and that all criticism whose object is only the book in question, and in which the author is judged according to that, is literary criticism" (Grosclaude, p. 149). The writers and critics involved in the personalities deplored by Malesherbes had obviously forgotten Baillet's initial premise that if one is free to write one is also free to criticize. In any case, the literary criticism of the middle decades of the eighteenth century was personality-ridden. It began with the differences between Voltaire and Fréron's predecessor, the abbé Desfontaines, after which it was Voltaire against Fréron; Fréron against Voltaire and the philosophes; Voltaire against Lefranc de Pompignan, La Beaumelle, and Rousseau; Palissot against almost everyone save Voltaire; Sabatier de Castres against the philosophes and Voltaire; and La Harpe against the antiphilosophes and later against the philosophes. In the midst of all this there was Rousseau against society; the Jansenists and a great many others against the Jesuits; and later on, as Robert Darnton has shown, the disestablished against the Enlightenment establishment, the lean and hungry Grub Street hacks against contented academicians.

In order to extract the critical essence from this imbroglio, one might put it that on the literary, as distinct from the ideological, level, the old Quarrel of the Ancients and Moderns persisted. Possibly the very idea of the Temple of Fame rendered this continuation unavoidable. While the moderns supposedly won the theoretical battle, their victory profited thought and science more than belles lettres; these, in spite of everything, remained based on the ideal of perfection. The writers of the Grand Siècle were allowed into the temple, but critics were not inclined to extend the same privilege to contemporaries, though writers and poets who created temples of taste did so. But the critics were not as easily persuaded. Thus eighteenth-century literary criticism in France was character-ized by two general traits concerning established models and their emulators: the dead were accorded generosity while a punctilious treatment was reserved for the living. These traits were accompanied by another, also observable in England: a general dissatisfaction with the present state of letters, which was contributed to by the exercise of comparing the age of Louis XIV to that of Louis XV. Not all living writers suffered by the comparison; indeed, some became instant entrants to the Temple of Fame. Voltaire is the most outstanding among those recognized as a classic (for the wrong works) in his time, and he had his apotheosis a few weeks before his mortal self definitely died. Crébillon, Marivaux, and even Gresset were also admit-ted to Parnassus, but significantly only because they could be assimilated to the company already there. The critical establish-ment was literally necessarily conservative, because the models belonged to the past. The critic's mentality thus could be lik-ened to that of a museum curator: he was a guardian and keeper, maintaining the standards of the temple and scrutiniz-ing works which were written as passports to immortality. One may say that criticism, beyond the personalities, resolved itself into a question of strict or loose interpretation of the rules of ad-mission. If practicing poets and writers like Perrault, Voltaire, and La Motte tended to be loose interpreters in their occasional criticism, a journalist like Fréron tended to be strict, as was Clément the critic, while some like Sabatier de Castres could be not only severe but partial. More was involved than differences of interpretation: the differences were between a creative tem-perament and a critical faculty, imagination against precedence, and, sometimes, the poet against the humanistic scholar.

If the distinction between what was and what was not literary criticism was unclear, so too was the distinction be-tween the writer and the man. This failure to distinguish was important because of the nature of eighteenth-century French society, especially the social role of decorum and the religious importance of moral conduct. The writer did not meet society only on the level of the Directorship of the Book Trade, but in the very requirements of style. To follow Buffon, style was the man; the man was judged through his work, and the work in terms of the man. The generally accepted tenet that literature and the arts ought to please and instruct afforded even more reason to confuse man and writer. Since writing also could be judged in terms of the reader's personal reaction, works could be and were described as flat, cold, tasteless, detestable, and disgusting—qualities which were transferred from the work to the author. Those who made a distinction between the content and the style of a work, or between the work and the writer, were rare indeed, and it is to the credit of Palissot, if indeed he did write the *Apollon Mentor,* that he made that distinction in regard to the novels of the younger Crébillon. The classical aesthetic posited an art of convention beyond the human, but writers and critics worked in the world, and personalities pierced through the polished surface of artistic conventions.

As a result of the linkings of moral values with literature, of writer and man, and the expectation that the man ought to live up to the moral values he professed, criticism often took the form of gossiping about the author, making libelous attacks on his person, and pointing to discrepancies between the man and the writer. News from the Republic of Letters thus tended at times to turn into the delights of scandalmongering. The world of authors and critics was filled with friction and tumult, a space far indeed from the quiet study or the serene heights of Parnassus.

### Desfontaines

For some of the writers of the early eighteenth century, one cause of friction and tumult was the much-maligned Abbé Desfontaines. His importance for the history of literary criticism in France lies in the fact that he laid to rest earlier negative views of the critic. Desfontaines himself, however, did not escape contempt, for the métier of critic was considered infamous. Nevertheless, the significance of his criticism was soon appreciated. As another critic, the abbé de La Porte, put it in the preface to his *Esprit de l'abbé Desfontaines* (1757): "One may say he was the creator of the type of criticism unknown before him, which had neither the cold dryness of analysis, nor the fastidious abundance of erudition spread without choice and on any occasion. A man like him was needed to avenge the honor of letters and oppose the progress of bad taste by heaping ridicule upon those works deserving it" (1:vii). It is not difficult to see why he made a great many enemies and why his name should have passed to posterity as an enemy of Voltaire and as the subject of a famous bon mot by the comte d'Argenson, then lieutenant of police and in charge of literary life and production. D'Argenson having called him in concerning a complaint against his criticism, Desfontaines explained that criticism was how he earned his living, and "One has to live." D'Argenson replied, "I don't see the necessity." The incident throws light upon the attitude towards the professional critic-journalist and the obstacles put in the way of all critics. Desfontaines was probably the first true literary critic as modern readers have come to understand that term; he was a professional of letters passing judgment upon books as they appeared. But to his contemporaries he was Aristarchus at the gate of the Temple of Fame.

Pierre François Guyot Desfontaines was born in Rouen on 29 June 1685, the son of a counselor to the Parlement, and of that class of men of the robe which produced a great many men of learning and letters in the seventeenth and eighteenth centuries. He studied the humanities with the Jesuits and did so well they induced him to join their order, which he did in 1700, taking holy orders in 1715 while finishing his philosophy course. He was then sent to Bourges to teach rhetoric. By then, however, Abbé Desfontaines had already had enough of teaching and of Jesuit life, and so, as the saying went, "he reentered the secular world." For several years Cardinal d'Auvergne was his patron, and he was even offered a parish which he soon gave up, preferring the life of letters to the priesthood. His opportunity for literary success came with his publication of the *Remarques historiques, philosophiques, et théologiques* (1722), written against the abbé Houtteville's *La Religion chrétienne prouvée par les faits*. Desfontaines collaborated with a

*99*

Jesuit who concerned himself with the substance of Houtteville's book, while Desfontaines made a critique of the style.

The following year he drew even more attention to himself by a short but sharp critique of one of the established writers of the day, Houdar de La Motte, whose play *Inès de Castro* was then having a great success. Desfontaines's critique was put in the guise of four points: 1) The tragedy of *Inès de Castro* is offensive to mores and deficient in verisimilitude; 2) Most of the verses in it are hard, flat, prosaic, and full of solecisms and barbarisms; 3) The author has shown in his preface that he writes poor prose; and 4) he has allowed his vanity to show and is too sour about his critics. To state such propositions about a successful play and an established writer was a sure way of making himself known. These *Paradoxes littéraires* of 1723 are also interesting for what they reveal about literary criticism and critics at the time. The critics chastise not only the style of a writer, but also his character; criticism is made to apply to morals, manners, style, grammar, linguistic usage, verisimilitude, and, as concerns drama, to the difference between the play as seen on stage and the play as read. In the case of Desfontaines and La Motte, the critic's point of departure is not the play as a success, but the will to argue. Criticism is a species of controversy. Criticism is also normative, for the critic presumes to tell the author how to write. One senses not only Desfontaines's pleasure in argument, but also the schoolmaster correcting the student's theme. But in addition, Desfontaines's *Paradoxes littéraires* was meant to proclaim the rights of criticism, and precisely of the new type he would exercise for the rest of his life, whose justification lay in an aesthetic concept and the belief in the Temple of Fame. This becomes obvious toward the end of the *Paradoxes,* when he dicusses *Inès de Castro* as seen and as written.

> Two things are incontestable: first, that the tragedy of *Inès* appeared very beautiful on stage; and second, that it appears today quite defective on paper. This is a unanimous judgment; it is therefore manifest that the acting of a great tragic actor makes for prestige, charm, and enchantment, and that one must be very circumspect about the public's applause.
>
> [P. 40]

*100*

Then why not judge a play as an action on a stage, not with a magnifying glass, but rather as a spectacle seen from the required perspective? That is an argument worth considering, Desfontaines admits, but if it is accepted, then the writer ought not to publish his play. This concession is then modified by a philosophical distinction concerning beauty. One type is external and merely appearance, as cloth might shine at a distance but be ugly close up, or like the shiny beauty of false diamonds. There are *beautés fardées,* cosmetic beauties. But there is another type.

> True beauty is intrinsic, and real beauty is independent of the point of view. A picture, if it be correct, is beautiful in itself, even though it must be seen in the light. For the picture is composed of color, and light is, so to say, intrinsic to its nature. But a work of the mind has no solid or true merit if it please but the distant eye, only charms the ear, and must fear the reflections of connoisseurs. Were it otherwise, the art of writing, and above all that of dramatic writing, would be reduced to mere quackery.
>
> [P. 41]

It seems obvious that with such distinctions and standards, most writers would not find easy access to the Temple of Fame. For the critic required the writer, in an imperfect world, to produce works worthy of a universe of values which may be characterized as extraterrestrial. The critic stood between the poet in the world and glory in posterity.

It was these early writings which brought Desfontaines to the attention of Bignon, who thought he would be just the man to edit and revitalize the moribund *Journal des savants,* which by 1723, according to the abbé de La Porte, was dominated entirely by doctors. It had become almost a catalogue of the diseases and ills besetting mankind and thereby practically unreadable. Desfontaines was not chosen for his erudition, nor his Latin and Greek, but to make the journal readable; he was selected for his writing ability and, eventually, his editorial skills. However, while the *Journal des savants* improved, Desfontaines made himself enemies. He was accused of sodomy, arrested, sent to Bicêtre, and extricated from the prison and the charge only because some friends, among them Voltaire, intervened. (Voltaire, of course, later became his enemy, a not uncommon turnabout given Voltaire's temperament and vanity.) Though he was exonerated, Desfontaines would no longer put up with the vexations caused by his confrères, and he quit the *Journal* in 1727 to live off his pen. He did not mix with many authors, save the well established who no longer needed to fear him. He was never unoccupied, for the time he did not spend on his reviews he used writing other works. As Anne-Marie Meunier de Querlon put it, defending Desfontaines against Voltaire: "The abbé Desfontaines, like some scholars and even some wits, will present posterity with a problem I shall not try to resolve. Poet, historian, grammarian, critic, he is everything a bibliographer would wish ·(*Lettre d'un avocat,* p. 12). His criticism he exercised in three periodicals: *Le Nouvelliste du Parnasse, ou réflexions sur les ouvrages nouveaux* (1731–32), a publication stopped by the police; *Observations sur les écrits modernes* (1735–43), amounting in all to thirty-three volumes and three sheets, the privilège being withdrawn in 1743; and *Jugements sur les écrits nouveaux* (1744–46), totaling eleven volumes in all, though the last two are the work of Mairault, according to the article on Desfontaines in Moréri's *Grand Dictionnaire historique.* The *Observations* was Desfontaines's most important journal. Besides getting the collaboration of the abbé Granet, also coeditor of the *Nouvelliste,* he had the good sense to hire Fréron, who learned his craft with Desfontaines. However, Desfontaines wrote more than criticism, as Meunier de Querlon observed and as his bibliography bears out. He adapted Jonathan Swift's *Gulliver's Travels,* wrote a historical novel, numerous brochures, and controversial pieces on both sides of the disputes between doctors and surgeons which shook the world of medicine. He also wrote the *Dictionnaire néologique des beaux-esprits du temps, avec l'éloge historique de Pantalon-Phoebus,* which first appeared in 1726 and to which was added, in the third edition of 1728, the "Relation de ce qui s'est passé à la réception de l'illustre messire Christophe Mathanasius à l'Académie française." The *Dictionnaire* had a great many editions in the eighteenth century, and is still well worth perusing. It is very informative concerning the changes occurring in the French language at the time, in part because Desfontaines's critical methods included scrutinizing the linguistic usages of his contemporaries and underlining their neologisms. The piece on Pantalon-Phoebus is made up entirely of these neologisms, which might be called the Newspeak of the period, and can be considered a species of verbal collage. He presumably was poking fun at La Motte, just as in the Mathanasius satire his target was Fontenelle's style. The critic thus espoused an ideal of fixity for the language, perfect in the age of Louis XIV, and castigated writers who changed it. The *Observations sur les écrits modernes* made him a host of enemies, for he censured both the mediocre and the well-established writers and was none too respectful towards the Academy. It was this liberty which shaped the general reputation of the critics of his time, for Desfontaines was feared as a rigid censor who could make or unmake a literary reputation.

Given this fear, it is not surprising that relations between writers in the world and critics at the gate of the Temple of Fame involved perpetual warfare, including open battle, raids, guerrilla tactics, espionage, propaganda, and renewed fighting after periods of seeming peace. It is not my intention to write a history of the relations between critics and writers; several such were indeed written in the eighteenth century, and of these, Abbé Irailh's *Querelles littéraires; ou, Mémoires pour servir à l'histoire des révolutions de la république des lettres, depuis Homère jusqu'à nos jours* (1761), describes the relations between Desfontaines and Voltaire, perhaps the greatest hater of critics of all times. Indeed, to mention Desfontaines today brings to mind posterity's characterization of him as the first of a long line of Voltaire's enemies, just as the mention of Fréron calls up the title of one of F. C. Green's essays, "Voltaire's Greatest Enemy." One of Desfontaines's accomplishments, by no means minor, was to be among the first to penetrate and define the literary and moral character of Voltaire, just as Fréron would later define him as *the* philosophe, the foremost writer of the philosophic party, building on the ground outlined by his master, Desfontaines.

The dispute and the hatred between Desfontaines and Voltaire began in earnest with the critic's review of *La Mort de César* and his identification of *L'Enfant prodigue* as Voltaire's work. Voltaire did not spare him in various pieces, such as the *Discours sur l'envie* or the *Epitre à M. le président Hénault,* but his great counterattack came with *Le Préservatif* of 1738. Desfontaines answered in kind in *Voltairomanie* (1738), which Theodore Besterman describes in his biography of Voltaire as "a sort of garbage-can in which he scraped up many of the most scurrilous things ever said or written about Voltaire" (*Voltaire,* p. 197). While Besterman's description is accurate, it must be pointed out that in our affluent world, garbage cans not only yield curious finds but also lend themselves to meditations upon the nature of human society. Certainly the *Voltairomanie* does. It is an interesting document on the literary mores of the early eighteenth century, and particularly on the Grub Street aspect of the age, but it also presents Voltaire as he was perceived by many of his contemporaries before he became the sage of Ferney. This is not Voltaire as philosophe, great humanitarian, defender of the Calas and other victims, nor as leader of what one historian has called the "party of Humanity," but rather Voltaire as a first-rate gutter fighter in Grub Street. In *Le Préservatif* he had taken the critic to task both for his mistakes in his journals and for his character, to which the clever Desfontaines replied with rhetorical questions. Even admitting all that Voltaire wrote about him was right, would that make Voltaire a great writer or a gentleman?

> Will he pass any less, among connoisseurs, as being ignorant of the theatre, where he has been applauded merely for the vain harmony of his pompous tirades and his satirical and irreligious daring? Will his *Henriade* be any the less a dazzling chaos, a poor tissue of worn and inappropriate fictions, in which there is as much prose as verse and more solecisms than there are pages? It is a poem without fire, without invention, without taste, without genius. Will his *Temple of Taste* be any less the production of a small mind puffed up with pride?
>
> [P. 35]

As for his *Histoire de Charles XII,* it is hardly history, but a

*104*

novel, and his *Eléments de la philosophie de Newton* have made him the laughing stock of France and England. But then, and he expresses a reproach continually made against Voltaire, "This savant is a prodigy. He has hardly studied the most prickly and extended matter for two days, than he has mastered it thoroughly, and is capable of giving lessons to the greatest masters" (p. 53). The reason for his prodigious activity was explained by Desfontaines in terms to be repeated by Fréron: "This Alexander of literature aspires boldly to the universal monarchy of letters." This aspiration to empire no critic would tolerate, for while they may have considered themselves guardians of the temple, they never forgot that they were also part of the Republic of Letters. The vanity of the poet was such as to make for dreams of empire; the critic's task was to remind all writers that they were human, all too human.

The Voltaire-Desfontaines feud has been clearly outlined by Thelma Morris in "L'Abbé Desfontaines et son rôle dans la littérature de son temps" (1961); it will suffice here to say that it was not only symptomatic of Voltaire's relations with his critics but also indicative of why the profession of critic was held in contempt. But another trait can be noted for most critics: they had been good students in the humanities. Desfontaines was an ex-Jesuit, and had been well taught to analyse, criticize, argue, attack and defend opponents. But Desfontaines's role in the Republic of Letters is important in another respect: the very form of his periodical criticism in the form of letters, reviewing works not only of savants for savants, but poetry, plays, novels, and belles lettres, as well as science, meant that criticism had quit the learned journals of the seventeenth century, quit the space of the library, to enter not just Grub Street, but a new, autonomous, public literary space. The critics were despised and damned by the writers, but it took critics to alter the literary space of the library. This truth becomes clear through the career of the greatest critic of the eighteenth century, Elie Catherine Fréron.

## Elie Catherine Fréron

I first learned about Fréron through the anthology of Otis Fellows and Norman L. Torrey, *The Age of Enlightenment* (New York, 1942), which is the wrong way. The only thing good about learning of Fréron this way is that he is inseparable from Voltaire. But unfortunately this approach means that one always perceives Fréron from a position defined as progressive, liberal, humanitarian, and humanistic, so that poor Fréron becomes the very incarnation of what is termed reactionary, which is to turn him into a caricature of evil, precisely what Voltaire wanted posterity to think of him.

Even today, with the publication of Jean Balcou's *Fréron contre les philosophes* (1975), positions are still being taken in much the same way as two centuries ago because of the way French literature of the eighteenth century has been taught and because the winners write history. Fréron still has inspired only a relatively short scholarly bibliography, though there are signs of growing interest and he seems to be earmarked for reconsideration. But it is unlikely, and hardly to be wished for, that we shall be edified by a hundred and more volumes of Fréron studies. The *Année littéraire,* which he edited from 1754 to his death, surely deserves as much scrutiny as the works of Voltaire, for Balcou has shown it is a mine of information on the eighteenth century even more than on the Voltaire-Fréron battle.

In fairness to Fréron, it is better to begin, not with a celebrated Voltaire quatrain, but with the account of his life and career given in letter 30 of 15 April 1776 in the *Espion anglais.* The writer of the letter refers to Fréron as "the famous critic," and explains that in preparing to write his article he sought for men of letters, including Fréron's enemies as well as friends. He would have liked impartial men even better, but he found few of them. According to his account, Fréron was born in 1718 in Quimper, and he claimed he was born a gentleman, though his family merely had a good background; his father was a goldsmith. Fréron always claimed he was related to Malherbe, the first truly classical poet of the early seventeenth century. He also never forgot he was a Breton. He was educated by the Jesuits, entered their order for a few months, and remained attached in spirit to the order throughout his life. Like many ex-Jesuits he remained dressed as a member of that society for some time before he appeared as a fop, and in his early years in Paris he was long known as the abbé Fréron. Later he referred to himself as the chevalier Fréron, then simply as Monsieur Fréron, and eventually, even more simply but also more famously, as Fréron. Through a relative from Quimper, the abbé de Boismorand, he was introduced to Desfontaines, who hired him to work on the *Observations sur les écrits modernes.* Voltaire later described Fréron's relationship with Desfontaines in a libelous poem called "Le Pauvre Diable."

> A man of heavy mien I did accost,
> Who filled his belly by his pen;
> He was a great skimmer of Helicon's mire,
> And for his frolics from Loyola chased.
> From Desfontaines's ass he was born a worm,
> And in all senses worthy of the source.
> A cowardly Zoilus and once ugly Giton,
> This beastly thing was called Jean Fréron.

Even before the death of Desfontaines, Fréron began to publish his own pamphlets, but his career as a journalist began in earnest with the *Lettres de Madame la comtesse de* ——— *sur quelques écrits modernes,* which began to appear in December 1745. Only nineteen sheets were published, but he had already begun to attack Voltaire's pretension to hegemony in the world of letters. These early ventures into criticism also provided the first occasion for a visit to prison at Vincennes for disrespect to the abbé de Bernis, a protégé of Madame de Pompadour. From this experience Fréron drew two lessons—protection in high places was valuable, and caution was a virtue. Therefore he frequented the salon of Madame de Graffigny, cultivated the duc d'Estouteville, a descendant of Colbert, and even succeeded in being looked upon with favor by Comte d'Argenson, director of the book business, and Berryer, the lieutenant of police responsible for enforcing the laws regulating books and publishing. Thus Fréron felt safe enough to start another periodical, the *Lettres sur quelques écrits de ce temps* (April 1749-January 1754). This was Fréron's first truly original and characteristic periodical, the earlier one having been but a first try. He announced his intention in the guise of a vision.

> The figure of criticism lately appeared to me in a dream. She was surrounded by a crowd of poets, orators, historians, and novelists. In one hand she held a cluster of arrows, in the other some laurel branches. Her aspect, far from inspiring fear, inspired confidence among the ignorant lovers of the learned sisters. They dared look her straight in the eye and seemed to defy her wrath. The indignant goddess showered them with arrows. Some writers, whose modesty heightened their talents, received laurels; several received both recompense and chastisement at the same time. This vision, sir, has given me the idea of these letters in which eulogy and censure will be equally dispensed.
>
> [Quoted in *L'Espion anglais,* 3:114–15]

The writer of the *Espion anglais* article thought Fréron's modest tone and profession of equanimity was a way to ingratiate himself with the literary world, but that Fréron knew very well that more was needed in that world than fairness. At that time one reader already disliked him, or at least would come to, because Fréron had all the characteristics Voltaire hated. He was an ex-Jesuit, he had begun with Desfontaines, he was a religious writer, and he promised to be an antiphilosophe. The writer's article is interesting in that it interprets Fréron's early career in terms of the battle between him and the philosophic party as it stood in 1776. While the skirmishing between Fréron and some philosophes, Jean-François Marmontel and Jean-Jacques Rousseau, did begin in the 1750s, the battle with Voltaire was more literary and had not yet become the full-scale ideological warfare of the 1760s and 1770s.

But as two years later Voltaire's return to Paris would preoccupy the journals, so in the *Espion anglais* of 1776 it is the Fréron-Voltaire feud which commands the article in question. There could be no doubt, thought the writer, that given these two men, there would be war, as there was for some thirty years. Who began the hostilities? The *Espion anglais* does not know. (We know it already began with Desfontaines.) But whoever it was, the reporter went on, once opened there would be no quarter. Fréron was soon to feel the strength of his enemy, for using his connections, Voltaire managed to get Fréron's new periodical suspended for some time in 1751. But Fréron could not contain himself for long. As an introduction to the review of a book on Ninon de Lenclos, he sketched a masterful literary portrait of Voltaire without once naming him, and then got his readers to laugh by imagining a scene in which Madame Denis, delegated by her uncle Voltaire, was sent to plead with Malesherbes to have such criticism, such "personalities," stopped.

> With tears in her eyes, the niece of Arouet
> To Director Malesherbes came to complain
> That a writer, of great Malherbe the nephew,
> Against our team had dared lash out.
> "How can you suffer," she asked the aedile,
> That every month this raging critic,
> On every occasion, his black heart's
> Venom on my poor uncle pours?"
> "But," replied the Director of Books,
> "Our critic has depicted as fiction
> This fanciful monster you think real."
> "Fanciful monster! the error's extreme,"
> The niece replied, "My lord, do read:
> That monster there is my very uncle."               [3:117]

Fréron's attacks against Voltaire, according to the *Espion anglais,* were somewhat muted after the first suppression of the *Letters* because he enveloped the entire philosophic party in his offensive. It in turn would give no quarter and also tried to have his later paper, the *Année littéraire,* suppressed. Indeed, the philosophic party even succeeded in infiltrating Fréron's lines of communication with the official world of the direction of the book trade, since the go-between for Fréron and the official censor (who remained anonymous, an arrangement arrived at between Fréron and Malesherbes) was one of their men. Fréron gave him the articles to be read by the censor, but he never delivered any which could be damaging to the philosophes; instead he returned them to Fréron for revision, thereby rendering the *Année littéraire* far less lively and interesting reading. It was only when Fréron himself saw Malesherbes about the return of a rather inoffensive article that the stratagem was discovered, for the censor, being shown the articles Fréron brought, swore he had never seen them. The *Espion anglais* does not mention this.

In general the article must be read with caution, for it accepts certain accusations against Fréron which originated with Voltaire and other enemies. For example, it assumes that he was venal, an accusation also leveled against Desfontaines. But Fréron did not have to be venal because he earned a great deal from the *Année littéraire* in its best years. At one time he also edited the *Journal étranger,* and with both journals his income was some 40,000 livres. The *Espion anglais* also repeats the charge that he learned his métier well and rapidly because he used collaborators to whom he paid miserly wages. The truth is, he was indefatigable and possessed his literature to his fingertips; he was as much a man of letters as Voltaire, and also an enlightened man who argued for the necessity of reforms in the social, economic, and even religious domains. He was, however, a great spender who was ever short of cash, for this Aristarchus was in his private life a lover of wine, dinners, and women; the Christianity he defended was not the kind that interfered with his genuine love of life. He rented an apartment in the rue de Seine in which, contemporaries report, the gilding alone cost 30,000 livres. He also possessed a lovely country house, and gave extravagant and lively dinners for which he paid dearly in another sense, as he suffered from gout, a disease which finally laid him to rest at the still young age of fifty-eight.

The *Espion anglais,* in reviewing Fréron's life and career, was right about one thing: what began as a quarrel between Fréron and Voltaire, as criticism moving from the writer to the person, later developed into an ideological quarrel of profound implications. The literary relationship between the two men reflects the whole development of French literature from the late 1740s to the triumph of philosophy in the 1770s and may also be described as symptomatic of profound alterations in the structure of the literary space of the Old Régime. While the fighting took place in the realities of and with the help of mercenaries recruited in, Grub Street, the issue implied changes in the space of the library as well as in that of the Temple of Taste. Voltaire's attempted revolution on Parnassus, his *Temple du goût* being his manifesto as well as opening skirmish, had failed. His reordering of literary values was accepted by no one, not by the Italian comedians who parodied him, not by Desfontaines, and not by Fréron; these last two would never let him live down his failure. But in the end Voltaire and his cohorts did win the battle, because they shifted their ground and directed their attacks upon new terrain, thereby creating a new literary space, one far vaster than the relatively well-defined spaces of the library and the Temple of Fame. By the time of Fréron's death, the entire literary scene had been changed, and his long fight with Voltaire and the philosophes signified the creation of a new world of literature that persisted until the revolution involving the cinema and television.

Fréron's view of Voltaire is best summarized in the *Année littéraire* of 30 December 1760, in a masterful literary portrait of Voltaire under the guise of an essay on the Persian poet Sadi. This work combines the character sketch of Voltaire with the views of others who had known Voltaire as a young man in the period of the Regency and the early years of the reign of Louis XV and had noted his drive for universality.

> From his tender youth on he burned with the insatiable desire to know and repeat everything; he had talent, the drive to work, and facility. He first conceived the noble design of surpassing all previous tragic poets. . . . Sadi thus composed dramas in which there are brilliant parts, sometimes pathetic scenes, or tender ones, and what are called tirades, but no unity; his style is loose, uneven, at once epic and familiar. There are beautiful scenes which are ill prepared, vitiated plots, wit, and no judgment. That is what can be said of Sadi's theatre.
>
> [1760, 8:336]

And so on and on. As for his celebrated epic poem, the *Henriade,* it was judged to be neither a poem nor an epic, but versified history devoid of invention and poetry and lacking in warmth.

But Voltaire-Sadi, having gone through these noble literary genres, also decided to enter other fields: "Our audacious writer, when he was almost forty-three, threw himself body and soul into philosophy, setting out to penetrate the sanctuary of nature and divine the enigma of our being—and finished by being hissed" (p. 336). From philosophy he turned to history, a branch of learning in which he is hardly to be trusted. But then, Fréron maliciously asked, who admires this man, and why? His style is such that he easily fooled a certain type of reader: "the ignorant and half-wits, more terrible for letters than even the ignorant, the type of reader which never takes the trouble to stop, think, and compare, judging in a sovereign manner of everything without having bothered to learn anything, or persons of the world who have but superficial views of their pleasures and vaudevilles; such was the idolatrous troupe of Sadi's admirers" (p. 338). He copied from everyone and ended up plagiarizing from his own works. It was a charge Fréron was always ready to back up, because as the editor of a journal reviewing old and new works he had a prodigious knowledge of letters. "We have more than twenty volumes of the works of Sadi, and there is not one which offers a new idea; he had imagination only in expression, which is to say that for him form was everything and matter nothing" (p. 339).

Five years later, reviewing a new book on Petrarch, and struck by the literary genre of the triumphs, Fréron imagines one for Voltaire, of which the closing description is not without a touch of cutting wit: "A crowd of young poets and apprentice philosophers would sing his praises and make the air resound with these acclamations: '*Glory, honor and health to the divine Voltaire, to that great man who knows so well how to imitate that he needs no talent to create. Vivat, vivat to the divine Voltaire*' " (*Année littéraire*, 1765, 2:7–8). At the end of the portrait, Fréron asks himself whether Sadi-Voltaire can be called a poet, a historian, or a philosopher? The answer is none of these; Voltaire was only a *bel-esprit,* only a wit. But he makes the most devastating summing up of Voltaire in a few words: *le second dans tous les genres*—"the second in all genres."

Voltaire was not the only target for Fréron, but he was the main one because, as Fréron saw it, he symbolized so much of what was wrong in the France of the eighteenth century. So too did the philosophes. But Fréron's fundamental ideological opposition to the philosophic party was not all which separated him from Voltaire, Diderot, d'Alembert, La Harpe, Marmontel, and many other lesser writers. This party was, Fréron thought, linked to other phenomena which he discerned very clearly from his editorial position: the vulgarization or democratization of letters, and the rising mass of unimportant books being published, the growing number of aspirants to literary glory. Fréron lived and wrote in a time of pronounced literary inflation, and he could just as well have written Chamfort's famous observation: "Most books today seem to have been written in one day with books read the night before." Thus, reporting in the *Année littéraire* of 1770 on the abbé de La Porte's *Porte-feuille d'un homme du goût; ou, L'Esprit de nos meilleurs poètes* (Paris, 1770), he wrote:

> Never has one created as little as in this century; but in compensation, never has one copied as much, and stupidly so; it might be acceptable if one were content to transcribe authors. But the compilers repeat each other, and if anyone were to assemble their pretended choices, he would run the risk of finding the same extracts twenty times over. The titles are generally the most cared-for aspects of these types of books; it is as if one competed for the most seductive posters: *The Treasure of Parnassus, The Secretary of Parnassus, The Portfolio of the Man of Taste.*
>
> [8:122]

The reason for this is that mediocrity thrives and multiplies. Assessing the literary situation of 1773, he asked himself who the six great French men of letters were and decided on Voltaire, Lefranc de Pompignan, Piron, Buffon, Gresset, and Jean-Jacques Rousseau. As for the others, they were "an insolent rabble of incurable mediocrities, having neither genius, soul, nor style" (1773, 1:5). Most of them were members of the philosophic party, intolerant of others and tending to sing their own praises. Yet they had been successful.

They have created a new literature, a new morality, a new civility, over which they have exclusive rights. They occupy all the avenues of Parnassus; they have posted vigilant sentinels whose orders are, as soon as an author shows himself, to cry out "Who goes?" And unhappy he who does not answer with the proper password: "Philosophe!"

In 1774 he elaborated on the same theme and linked the novel phenomenon of young writers dashing off a piece without effort, thought, knowledge, or correction to the influence of Voltaire. "M. de Voltaire is the idol of young people who read only him, love only him, and swear only by him" (1774, 1:10). They imitated his worst features and disdained the critics who might help them perfect their work. But even worse was the patronage of letters which, as Fréron points out, had become fashionable. "Nothing is more noxious to letters than patronage [*le protectorat*]. I call thus the mania for 'protecting' a writer so prevalent in our day. There is a furor to be a Maecenas as there is to be an author. One becomes infatuated of some weakly writer; he is admired, extolled; and one would like to do something out of nothing; one is not God" (p. 10). This somewhat explained the success of writers like Suard, Thomas, La Harpe, Chamfort, and even Marmontel. But Fréron also spoke of his own experience.

> I could, sir, cite myself as proof of the astonishing facility with which the capital allows itself to be prepossessed. In 1744 I wrote a rather poor ode, "The Conquests of the King." I recited the strophes as I finished them to some friends, who memorized them and repeated them to others. Soon my ode was the talk of all Paris. Everyone asked for readings and I could not answer all the invitations I received. I was gratified with eulogies as if Pindar, Horace, Malherbe, or Rousseau were but schoolboys next to me. Prault, bookseller and printer on the quai Conti, now on the quai des Gèvres, hearing this rapture of unanimous applause, hurried to get hold of so precious a piece; he bought it high and fortunately did not lose by it. The craze was such that he printed three editions in a week; my supposed masterpiece even had the honor of being counterfeited in the provinces and abroad.
>
> [1770, 1:147–48]

Finally, writers had themselves become men of the world,

114

elegant men about town, attending parties and dinners and dressing like fops. This was a far cry from the seventeenth-century life of letters, when writers hardly showed themselves in society, instead spending their lives in study, meditation, the pursuit of knowledge, and the perfecting of their craft.

Balcou's *Fréron contre les philosophes* brings out clearly the "party" aspect of the philosophes and their intolerance. They captured the bastions of the Republic of Letters, and by 1770 it was Fréron who was persecuted, harassed, vilified, and spied on. Twentieth-century readers tend to think of the result of this battle as light triumphant over superstition, liberalism over reaction, and enlightenment over prejudice, they have in effect accepted the philosophic party's own version of the battle. This party was an interest group, and like other corporate bodies of the Old Régime, it acted in its own interest and for its own privileges. One wonders whether its action was not an attempt to transform the profession of letters and its practitioners precisely into a legally recognized "grand corps de l'Etat," a writers' corporate body with privileges like other bodies. The philosophes may have begun as an antiestablishment party, but by the death of Louix XV they had become the literary establishment.

Fréron stood for law, religion, and country, but also for necessary reforms, and on the aesthetic level for taste as conceived along the lines of established literature, though he knew well enough to distinguish between copying and imitation and never ceased calling for living literary works rather than imitations. Like many other critics, he felt his century to be sadly lacking in great works and perceived it as petty, trivial, and ignoble. It was frequently clever and witty, but not great compared to the previous age. Such a jaundiced view of one's own time may be a hazard of being a professional critic, but his opinion is not for all that invalidated. It is amusing to speculate upon how he would be considered today in the weedy groves of Academe if the Revolution had been avoided by a judicious and energetic Louis XVI. Would Fréron be the French department's Dr. Johnson?

## Literature as a Consumer Item

Fréron's complaints about the state of letters were not unfounded, but they were grounded on moral and aesthetic considerations; he condemned pretension, mediocrity, and lack of creativity. But there is another way of describing his reaction: he perceived, without formulating it as such, the transformation of literature into a consumer item. Grub Street had turned into the marketplace. Publishers enriched themselves, writers increased in numbers and diminished in price, and literature became mere fashion. To be sure Grub Street had always been a marketplace where one sold one's pen because one could afford neither morality nor aesthetics. But it also implied marginal activity and a restricted, limited market, in contrast to the broader vistas inherent in the noble concept of literature. But by the 1750s in Paris, by sheer weight of production, Grub Street seemed to some to have become literature itself. La Bruyère's remark that it is an art to write a book, intended to distinguish the true writer and his art from the mere amateur, had in a sense been turned against him. It had become all too easy to write a book, and the métier had become so commonplace that one could ask, "Who doesn't write?" This new situation could be the occasion for humor as well as for polemics.

A small duodecimo of 1755 by Rémond de Saint-Sauveur entitled *Agenda des auteurs* is a fine example of the satirical and humorous approach to the new literary marketplace. It is a cross between a dictionary and an almanac, in which the author proposes to teach how to write a book, for everyone writes these days. "Today one writes to make a name, for employment, even for a living" (p. 17). The form of the work itself is a demonstration of its intention and content. It begins with a dedicatory epistle to an academy, which is followed by a foreword and announcements by the editor, printer, stitcher (*brocheur*), binder, and bookseller (*colporteur*). These are supplemented by an advice to the reader, preliminary discourse, preface, and finally, the smallest part of the book, the writer's agenda. The appendices include an "Approbation of Argus,"

"Approbation of the Friends of the Writer," and a long section of "Errata raisonné" referring the reader to errors in the title, dedication, foreword, announcements, advice to the reader, preliminary discourse, preface, body text, approbations, and the errata itself, though the book ends with a privilège granted by Apollo. The theme is given at the end of the book by the god himself, who observes "that it is very easy to be an author, that a book is made in one day, printed the second, sold the third, and forgotten the fourth; so that it is easy to start over" (p. 210).

The book is a lovely trifle, and most informative about the book business, even, in some respects, for a bewildered modern author. In the editor's advice the reader is told, for example, what editors do. The editor explains that he chose the duodecimo, an ordinary and commodius format, that the impression is fine, the paper of good quality, that there are few errors in spelling, and no nonsense or equivocal passages. He has eliminated what could not be understood and suppressed what could be too easily understood, and the book requires neither notes, remarks, nor a key to divine the true meaning. From the printer we learn that he knows neither how to read nor to write, but his illiteracy does not matter. Printing is a business: one buys the goods, sets up the machinery, and gets someone to run the establishment. The writer brings his manuscript; the *prote* or foreman in charge of printing takes over; proofs are run; the author corrects them; the book is printed. If the author is fashionable, it sells; if not, the store fills with blackened paper which is sold by the pound to grocers. In the meantime the publisher is a man about town and grows rich, and one publisher is richer than another only because he has more editions of the same book, or because he publishes prohibited books or Latin prayer books. But, the publisher adds, because we poor publishers are being ruined, what is needed is more and more books. So go to it, writers, produce novelties! The stitcher thinks the book need not be bound because it is a useful catalogue, and published incognito, and can be sold under cover by almost anyone: a waiter, a toilet attentant, or a ragpicker. Anybody sells books these days, and this book can be carried anywhere; therefore it should be softbound. The binder, of course, thinks the book must be bound because it is the binding which really sells the book: "Ornamentation and the cover are the guarantees of success" (p. 20). For this particular item, he explains, he has chosen the finest morocco leather of the Levant in various colors: saxon green, true purple, clear lemon, even rose, paler than those books of hours bound for ladies of distinction.

The bookseller explains that his job is obscure, because it is risky to sell books without a privilège, but these are really good books, the proof being that they sell well and at high prices—without even being looked at. On the ground floor of the theatre, along the quais, or at the church door, an ambulant bookseller waits to distribute the elixir of literature and the true medicine for boredom.

The preface is concerned with how to write prefaces even for a useless book, and in the body text one learns: "Today being an author is an estate, like being a soldier, magistrate, churchman, or financier" (p. 63). But though authorship is recognized as a separate état, everyone wants to write. This confusion in the Republic of Letters, however, merely reflects that of the nation itself, which is all to the good since it demonstrates the high value put on wit. Of course, the profession of writing differs from others in that one does not need special training or to create a masterpiece to be accepted into it. "I wanted to be an author, such was my vocation; I dared to be one, that was my apprenticeship; I am one, such is my masterpiece" (p. 68). It suffices, to be an author, to place one's name at the head of any work whatsoever. The first thing to do is to choose a title, which is not as easy as one may think, for it must attract the reader. It ought to be new, striking, and astonishing, such as *Le Code de la nature,* or *Ah, quel conte!* Second, an author must be novel and daring, not simply following in the footsteps of tradition, but giving the reader a system of the world, revealing the secrets of human nature, and so on. This section of the *Agenda des auteurs* is filled with allusions to contemporary writers such as the abbé d'Houteville, Father Berruyer, Buffon, La Mettrie, Maupertuis, Condillac, Duclos, d'Alembert, Voltaire, and Raynal, so that the centerpiece of Saint-Sauveur's construction turns out to be a commentary on the books of his time as a species of product. One sells *Le Code de la nature* as any commodity, and literary production is surveyed in terms of a market. Saint-Sauveur is saying: look at what sells; produce what sells; the market bears anything from epics to bagatelles. The spirit of the author comes out when his censor writes that he has read, or rather looked at, the present volume and found it may be published, for he has seen nothing which is unusual or different from what may be found in other books—to wit, useless things, antitheses, epigrams, and much wit. An author will find what he wants to read, and he who is not one will learn how to be. But the book ought to be prohibited to persons of good sense and those disgusted with literary novelties. Saint-Sauveur in this lovely spoof succeeds by laughing at himself as well as the new Grub Street.

Simon Nicolas Henri Linguet's *L'Aveu sincère; ou, Lettre à une mère sur les dangers que court la jeunesse en se livrant à un goût trop vif pour la littérature* (London and Paris, 1768), a short polemical piece, deals with the same phenomenon but is addressed to a different public than Saint-Sauveur's book, and is also informed by an entirely different spirit. Far from being a charming trifle which throws light upon the literary scene, it is a pessimistic analysis of the situation of the man of letters as well as a polemic against the philosophes. Under the pretext of writing to a sister with growing children, Linguet warns against the danger of literature: it can lead only to misery. Above all, do not push children towards that arid rock on which literary glory, it is said, has established her temple. Linguet regards the Temple of Fame as an entirely false attraction and a temple of despair. It is as if the myth of literary glory were being dispelled and shown to be a nefarious illusion.

"What is the life of a man of letters?" asks Linguet. It is sown with barbs even if his ashes are crowned with flowers. "His glory is the result of his falls. One moment suffices to dishonor him, and it takes ages to glorify him" (p. 24). Even if a good work is produced, its destiny is but to amuse a small circle of the leisured and compromise its author. Anyone who sets out to write must be prepared to be persecuted or to blush. There is a creative pleasure in writing, but the métier of a man of letters is not restricted to the pleasures of his study and writing table. The writer wants to publish; the approval and friendship of a small circle of admirers will not satisfy him. The bitterness comes when the writer seeks a publisher; it is then that the illusions are dissipated and the truth will out. "Literature today has become a veritable financial operation: it is a continuous brokerage, talk of sales and resale, a market-place in which more use is made of calculations than genius" (pp. 37–38). There is nothing more sad and humiliating to the young unknown author than trying to sell his manuscript to a publisher. But what happens after he has overcome the disdain and his book is published? There is a happy moment for the author: he holds his child in his hands and marvels at it, and he reads and looks at the first copy with delight. But happy the author whose book creates an uproar, a controversy, discussion, for at least it is read; in most cases a first book is never followed by a second edition. To avoid this common fate an author seeks to sell his work by intrigue, by the prestige bestowed upon him by high patronage, and so sacrifices his quiet, honor, or both. The truth is that books need to be supported and pushed forward, because merit alone won't make for success in the world. One must flatter, submit to humiliation, bear mockery and disdain, and remember that this is the way to make a reputation. "An author become famous has almost always begun by being the plaything of those circles which later extol him" (p. 46). It is rarely during his lifetime that a writer can enjoy the admiration he prompts; he usually earns merely ingratitude.

Good and useful works, books with a moral and instructive purpose, are received coldly and sometimes with positive displeasure. Linguet's arguments are the same as those of Rameau's nephew, who thought mankind did not wish to be lectured, but he also strikes a rather original note, for he ties writing and literature with melancholia. "The first fruit of literature, and most certainly for those who practice it, is this languor of the soul, this cruel poison known as ennui, which imperceptibly gnaws at it. It thrives among the cultivated as migraine does among those of delicate constitution. It undermines them, and dries them out with as much cruelty as the slowness of its work" (p. 61). Worse yet, literature is not only a poison for the individual as man of letters, but also for the nation; because peace, liberty, and virtue are the fruit of ignorance supported by poverty and the love of humble and arduous work. The richer a nation becomes, the less virtue, liberty, or peace there is, for riches beget luxury and the leisure of the sciences, and from these is born philosophy. Linguet means "philosophy" in the late eighteenth-century sense of the term, what Fréron called *la philosophaille,* and both were referring directly to the growing numbers and strength of, and fashion for, the philosophes. The book ends like one of Rousseau's diatribes against learning, letters, and luxury, all of which Linguet sees as part of the same phonomenon of philosophy, the cause and symptom of decadence.

Linguet's total rejection of literature and philosophy is in part to be explained by his generally paradoxical views of society, but also by the new presumption shown by men of letters, and especially by those who called themselves philosophes, a presumption which followed a reassessment of the man of letters in society. For that elusive type had at last chosen to regard himself and his role in positive terms. He had become so fashionable that he had ended by considering himself of a noble essence.

# 4

## The Philosophes; or, The Space of the New Elite

*To be a great man in letters, or at least make a revolution which will be noticed, one must, as in the realm of politics, find the ground prepared and be born at the right time.*

Chamfort

After forty-five years he had finally done it, despite the critics, despite his enemies, despite the king, despite the church. He had achieved that universal empire over letters that Desfontaines and Fréron claimed he had sought all along, and his return to Paris was a veritable triumph, like a prince visiting a city. In February 1778, the *Anécdotes secrètes pour servir à l'histoire de la république des lettres en France depuis 1762 jusqu'à nos jours* were full of Monsieur de Voltaire's return to Paris. On 12 February the journal reported that Monsieur de Voltaire had remained in his dressing gown and nightcap all day long the day before, receiving the court and the town in that attire; he excused himself by explaining he was very tired and incommodated. He always spoke of going to bed but never went. There was a regular ceremonial to these visits to Voltaire. Callers were introduced into a suite of superb apartments, and the marquise de Villette, mistress of the hôtel, and Madame Denis, Voltaire's niece, did the honors. A valet informed Voltaire of all the callers who came; the marquis de Villette and the comte d'Argental presented those he did not know personally or had forgotten; he received their compliments, answered by a polite word or two and returned to his study to dictate the corrections for his tragedy *Irene* to his secretary (1:114–15). And when Voltaire became ill, the

122

*Anécdotes secrètes* reported on his illness as the marquis de Dangeau had formerly reported in his diary every little ill of Louis XIV. Monsieur de Voltaire is constipated; Monsieur de Voltaire sent for Dr. Tronchin, who told him to go to bed and take a rest; Monsieur de Voltaire found he was unable to urinate today; Monsieur de Voltaire, having walked too much, found his legs swollen and again sent for Dr. Tronchin, who again told him to take to bed and stay there; none of which kept him from overworking his secretary Vagnières.

Voltaire's return and triumph was symbolic of the victory of the philosophic party over public opinion. The *Anécdotes secrètes* report that the devout party and the clergy were powerless against this impious man of letters, and that even the Parlement could not have acted against him. "Fanaticism is thus reduced to muted intriguing on the one hand, crying scandal on the other, and universally suffering the sojourn of this Apostle of Incredulity" (1:147). When the great man fell seriously ill, both the *parti dévôt* and *parti philosophique* were interested in how he would go. Voltaire thus became, at the end of his life, the very example of human destiny: after the glory came the diseases of old age, but the old man fooled them all again and recovered to go to the Comédie française, where he was acclaimed by the crowd which precipitated itself towards him to touch him and try to catch some hair from his fur lining. Voltaire had turned into a species of lay saint, and was crowned an immortal even before his final departure. What a pity Fréron was not there to see it and report on it. There was enough of what Americans aptly called "ham" in it to make a good article for the *Année littéraire*.

Voltaire's apotheosis was made possible by his persistence, his longevity, his great sense of public relations, the very agitated life he had led, and his capacity for remaining the object of attention, talk, scandal, and controversy. But it was also due to a reevaluation of the role of the writer or man of letters in society. After the long period of relative obscurity, contempt, or grudging acceptance, the man of letters was about to earn his place in society and history. Only a few did, but they sufficed to change society's notions. This "surfacing" of men of letters

*123*

may have resulted from the noise they made, but it was aided by the fact that the priests and those exercising secular power cut poor figures because of their quarrels and corruption. This rethinking of the nature and function of the man of letters may be perceived as early as Charles Duclos's *Considérations sur les moeurs de ce siècle* (1st ed. 1751), but one may also trace the progress of this revisionism in the annual discourses proposed by the Académie française for the prize in eloquence: in 1753, "Love of Letters Inspires Love of Virtue"; in 1761, "The Charm of Study," a poetry prize which went to Marmontel; in 1761, "The Fate of Poetry in This Philosophical Age," the prize for this essay going to Chabanon; and in 1765, "The Poet," for which the nonpoetic La Harpe wrote an epistle, Chamfort a philosophical discourse entitled "The Man of Letters," Mercier a poem on "Genius," and an author called Fontaine a "Discourse on Philosophy." In 1770 the subject was still in fashion, and two items were proposed: "Epistle to a Young Man Who Would Cultivate Letters" and another "Epistle to Men of Letters." In 1772, one Doigny Du Ponceau proposed an "Epistle to a Celibate Man of Letters" filled with edifying verses in favor of marriage, citizenship, and the consolations of having a wife and children in your old age. It is pure Greuze, and philosophy with sentiment.

> The true sage serves and consoles humanity,
> His entire being to society he devotes,
> And turns not from him the cherished partner
> Who helps him bear the burdens of life.

What a lack of skepticism after Bayle, Baillet, and Fontenelle, as if a cherished partner could not turn into one of life's burdens. But the same year also saw an "Epistle of a Young Poet to a Young Warrior," and 1775 brought La Harpe's "Advice to a Young Poet" and, once more, Doigny Du Ponceau with "The Dignity of Men of Letters," which upon examination turns out to be a history of men of letters in a nutshell and a eulogy of them as bearers of light. For Doigny Du Ponceau the man of letters is the noblest of men.

> The most noble of mortals is the mortal who thinks,
> Jealous to keep his noble independence,

*124*

> The noble's corrupting succor he rejects,
> Who for his patronage debasement expects.

And unlike the nobleman who founds his prestige on his ancestors, the man of letters is his own creation.

> It is not asked, when he appears,
> From which ancient source
> His life, rank, and blood do flow.
> Himself he has created and nothing owes to chance.
> His just renown o'er a hundred leagues before him spreads,
> And over the unknown crowd he's raised,
> And from him, blushing, turn the great,
> Who but for glorious ancestors
> Would not oblivion have escaped.

The verses are mediocre, but the thought is not without a historical interest since nobility is being transferred from the feudal class to the self-made man of letters. It is already the voice of Figaro telling Almaviva: "Because you are a great lord you think you are a genius! . . . You took the trouble to be born, and nothing more." If the old nobility rests its prestige on its past, the man of letters commands the future. Immortal, animated by noble enthusiasm, he survives in and through his writings, and his ambition rules the future. As an example the poet cites Voltaire, who earned a statue while he still lived. Voltaire's glory serves as an example of what the man of letters may earn if he puts himself in the service of mankind and virtue. His high calling compels him to be an example of virtue and moral greatness, for the eyes of the world are ever upon him.

> Recall, the universe, unceasing, looks to you,
> And to better instruct it, its example you must set.

Men of letters should unite in a common cause, surmounting petty quarrels, envy, and jealousy, and join in love and friendship, for only the virtuous will enter the Temple of the Muses, only the virtuous enter the Temple of Fame, only the philosophes occupy Parnassus. And Fenélon is joined to Voltaire as an example of the new type of man of letters.

> You were great at the court and upon Mount Parnassus,
> Simple in favor and firm in disfavor,

And the peace, virtue, and felicity of man,
Your heart's last wishes were.

Doigny's poem was thought worthy of publication; it is a fine example of the transformation which had occurred in letters and of how one could flatter the philosophic party and Monsieur de Voltaire. The view of the man of letters presented here may be referred to as lyrical, and is a central point of the transformation: the man of letters was endowed with a mission; he was no longer a man of study and meditation, writing books and trying to keep his head above water in the difficulties of a flooded Grub Street. His goal was nobler, less selfish: it was the enlightenment of humanity. He had left his study for the forum and his quartos and folios for a torch.

The ideas expressed in Doigny's poem were not original; they had been in the air for some time and have a definite affinity with the views Louis Sébastien Mercier expressed in *Le Bonheur des gens de lettres* of 1766. In Mercier's imagination the man of letters assumes the sacred office described and discussed in Paul Bénichou's *Le Sacre de l'écrivain* (Paris: Corti, 1973). Bénichou begins with Mercier; the views of the sacred mission of the writer he advances do not find their full expression until the nineteenth century, though there is no denying their origin in the years 1760–70.

The pretensions and presumptions of the new breed of writers, discerned and denounced by Fréron, are clearly set forth in Mercier, La Harpe, Chamfort, d'Alembert, and Diderot, though with varying degrees of megalomania. Their vision rests on a theory of historical progress in which men of letters are perceived as having been the instruments of that progress which has led up to the Enlightenment and the philosophic party. The view is well set forth in the second part of d'Alembert's *Discours préliminaire de l'Encyclopédie,* and it was repeated later on by Madame de Staël and others. Mercier puts it succinctly in his *Bonheur des gens de lettres:* "If thought be useful to mankind, we owe [men of letters] everything; they have put out the fires of fanaticism, polished the mores of nations, prepared the way to great discoveries; they do not judge the world, but enlighten it in silence" (p. 8). Mercier restated similar views with more vigor and confidence in *De la littérature et des littérateurs* (1778), where he sees the writer as a legislator of mankind, and his influence as an estabished and irreversible fact. "The influence of writers is such that today they may announce their power and not disguise the legitimate authority they exercise over the minds of men. Firm upon the base of public interest and the true knowledge of man, they will direct national ideas; private will is in their hands" (p. 9).

With Mercier one has moved beyond the world of the older generation of philosophes like Voltaire and even Diderot. They had been born within the literary space of the library and drawn and fascinated by the vision of Parnassus, but Mercier is already a man of the Revolution, of a new mystique and a social mathematics. One thinks of Condorcet as well as the visions and social catechism of Volney, and of the poetic-architectural elucubrations of Claude-Nicolas Ledoux. But the triumph of philosophy implied also a rejection of the old erudition and its literary space, the library, so that Mercier's fictional visit to the Royal Library in the year 2440 (as told in *L'An 2440, rêve s'il en fût jamais* [Paris, 1771]) is most revealing. The consciousness men of letters had of themselves originally was inseparable from books and libraries; one might even argue that the rise of literary history up to the triumph of the philosophes and the theory of progress is inseparable from libraries and the particular types of men associated with them. But a new theory of genius was concomitant with the reevaluation of the man of letters and the triumph of the philosophes. The writer with a sacred mission is a genius, apart from humanity, plunged in profound thought; only such a man can lead mankind from the darkness to the light, from error to truth. And genius does not need books. Therefore the Royal Library of 2440 was a far cry from the marvel housed in the Hôtel de Nevers in the rue de Richelieu. The two hundred thousand books it housed had been reduced to a handful. As the librarian explains: "We have abridged the best: the whole has been corrected according to the true principles of morals" (1785 ed., 1:188). The library has shrunk to a small reading room with a few volumes—so few, indeed, that it is possible to list what remains and what has been eliminated or abridged. Homer, Sophocles, Euripides, Demosthenes, Plato, and Plutarch remain among the Greeks, but Herodotus, Sappho, Anacreon, and Aristophanes have been burned. In Latin literature Virgil, Pliny, Titus Livius, and Sallust are intact, but Lucretius survives only in extracts, Cicero has been shortened, Ovid and Horace expurgated, Seneca reduced by three-fourths, Tacitus can be read only with special permission, Catullus and Petronius have disappeared, and Quintilian has been reduced to one volume. English literature survives in the most volumes, including Milton, Shakespeare, Pope, Young, and Richardson; as for Italian letters, there is the *Jerusaleme liberata* and Beccaria's work on crimes and punishments. French literature has also been sharply censored and cut: Descartes, Montaigne, and Charron remain, but Malebranche, Arnauld, Nicole, Bourdaloue, and Pascal are all out; Fénelon's *Telemachus,* the abbé de Saint-Pierre, Corneille, Racine, Molière, and Crébillon have survived the purge. La Fontaine has been reduced to a few fables, as have also La Motte and de Nivernois. A few poems of J. B. Rousseau survive, as do the *Henriade,* some prose, and a few tragedies of Voltaire. J.-J. Rousseau, however, is there in his entire work, as well as *L'Esprit des loix, L'Histoire naturelle, De l'esprit, L'Ami des hommes, Bélisaire,* the works of Linguet, the discourses of Thomas, St. Servan, Dupaty, and Le Tourneur, the *Entretiens sur Phocion,* and the *Encyclopédie,* reorganized along a better plan. Historical writings have generally been drastically reduced to become the lives of great men. This is literature according to philosophy, and bears out Fréron's vituperations against the triumphant dryness of the philosophic view of letters. The reduction is also interesting in that it recalls Voltaire's standards in the *Temple du goût.* But Voltaire perceived poets perfecting their work, and the reduction was effected in the name of aesthetic principles never fully attained in the sublunary world. It was artistic and literary reduction presided over by taste. But the fire which reduced the Royal Library to a small reading room (and Mercier mentions no readers) was a moral fire. Thus in 2440 one will no longer be in a literary space at all.

Fortunately the Bibliothèque royale survived the reveries of this would-be Savonarola and its successor, the Bibliothèque nationale, became a true refuge for letters and men of letters even during the Revolution. Franz Blei, a German-Czech writer, tells the marvelous story of the eccentric utopian Count von Schlabrendorf, who quit reading and got mixed up in politics during the Revolution, chanced to escape the guillotine, and promptly returned to the Bibliothèque nationale, never to leave its shelter again. One is also reminded of Paul Valéry's answer during the occupation of Paris to a German officer who, seeing him leave the Collège de France, asked what it was. The poet answered: "It is a place where the spirit is free." The literary space of the library was not without its quarrels and pettiness, but as Baillet had defined it, it was the space of the free spirit because it was the space of writers and their readers as critics. When one thinks of Mercier's future national library, one cannot help but agree with Fréron that it was the philosophes who had become fanatical. But, of course, this merely brings up the old question of whether the philosophes were true philosophers or merely another set of men of letters who had gained their hegemony by the antiphilosophical devices of intrigue, cabal, and self-praise.

The lyrical interpretation of the man of letters saw a seer and a sacred mission, but more sober reassessments survived. The negative satirical image was a thing of the past, but the positive image did not have to be that of a genius leading the people to victory over fanaticism and oppression. The man of letters was first discerned as a new social type.

In his very successful *Considérations sur les moeurs de ce siècle* (1751), Charles Duclos discussed the man of letters with reference to other conditions in society. It is obvious that he had become a figure in the world, for otherwise there would have been no need to define him socially. Duclos of course was a man of letters himself, but unlike the savants and poets of the previous century, he was not defending letters for other men of letters or defining him from a position of social inferiority, or from within the limits imposed by the literary space of the library. His public was *le beau monde,* nonprofessionals, not other scholars. Literature, in short, already existed as a social phenomenon with a body of readers who read for pleasure, and without being occupants of the space of the library or citizens of the Republic of Letters. They were likely to be readers of Desfontaines or Fréron. Duclos recognized that being a man of letters was an état for those who did not have one, a position in society for those who otherwise would have had no position.

Duclos himself was a case in point. Born in Dinan in 1704, of parents who were in the business of men's hats but also had interests in iron works, he was left much to himself, sent to Rouen at six to learn the rudiments of education with a sister, and then sent to Paris at nine, going first to a gentleman's school where he met the chevalier d'Aydie, who presented him to the important Brancas family. He entered the Collège d'Harcourt in 1718, where he did well in rhetoric; he returned to Dinan for a short time and then went back to Paris under the pretext of studying law, but instead attended fencing lessons, frequented rakes and poets, and generally had a good time until his mother called him back when she heard how he studied. He soon returned to Paris, this time really to study law, though he rather neglected it for literature, going to the theatre and meeting writers at the Café Procope, which was then frequented by Boidin, the abbé Terrasson, Fréret, Du Marsais, La Fage, and Baron. (The Gradot, the other literary café, was the favorite of La Motte, Saurin and Maupertuis.) Duclos, still having done nothing, was a social success and frequented some of the best salons of Paris, including those of Madame Staal-Delaunay, Madame de Tencin, Madame Du Deffand, Helvétius, and d'Holbach. He also had ties with the Brancas, the actress Mlle. Quinault, Madame d'Epinay, and Madame de Pompadour, and it was thanks to such relations that in 1739 he was named to the Académie des Inscriptions et Belles Lettres without having written anything. One may say he was a man of letters even before he was a writer. Mlle. Quinault left him 10,000 livres in her will; Madame de Pompadour got him named historiographer royal with a stipend of 18,000 livres; he also had some connection with the manuscript division of the Royal Library and was a friend of the then influential Cardinal de Bernis.

In short, Duclos, although without a social situation in the usual sense of the term, was a well-connected young man. He was even named mayor of Dinan in 1744, a position he took seriously, embellishing the city and getting it subsidies from the Crown treasury; he was also a deputy to the Estates General of Brittany. In 1745 he began to think of the Académie française. By then he had written three works: *La Baronne de Luz; Les Confessions du comte de* ———— ; and the *Histoire de Louis XI*. But it was not necessary in those days to be a veritable man of letters or writer to be part of the Academy. Duclos entered in 1746 and immediately showed what he was capable of, for in his acceptance speech this man who had not written much nevertheless proclaimed that the Academy was the preserve of men of letters, that all Academicians were equal, and that writers were persons of independence. He soon became the leader of the men of letters in the Academy, and when in 1755 he was made perpetual secretary, he played a major role in reforming the Academy by favoring the candidacy of men of letters. He died in 1772, a rich man with a fortune of 260,000 livres. He also had become a major figure in the literary establishment which was not yet that of the philosophes. It is thus no wonder that Duclos should be among the first to define that curious status, man of letters. He perceived the importance of the Académie française as the institution through which men of letters could become part of the establishment, gain a prestigious position in society, and efface the old negative image. The Academy was to become the bastion of the literary circle. The task which was begun by Duclos was completed by d'Alembert, so that the Academy did finally belong to letters, but letters as philosophy.

In his *Considérations,* Duclos is aware that a change has occurred in the relations of writers and society.

> In former times men of letters given to study and writing for their contemporaries thought only of posterity. Their candid and rugged manners had no relation with those of society; and the men and women of society, less educated than today, ad-

mired their works, or rather their names, without thinking of being capable of living with them. There was perhaps even more consideration than repugnance in this distance.

[P. 211]

Duclos believed that progress in the sciences had changed this situation so much that in his day individuals affected learning and society sought out men of letters and scholars, an exchange which worked to the benefit of both. D'Alembert later was less sure about the benefits men of letters could expect from frequenting society. As he wrote in his "Essai sur la société des gens de lettres et des grands": "It is not at the Hôtel Rambouillet that Descartes discovered the application of algebra to geometry, nor at the court of Charles II that Newton discovered universal gravity; as for the manner of writing, Malebranche, who lived in retirement and whose amusements were children's games, is nonetheless a model for philosophical prose" (*Mélanges de littérature, d'histoire, et de philosophie,* 1:383). But Duclos was not the equal of the men d'Alembert used as examples in this passage, and for Duclos the *grand monde* had done wonders. Men of letters had, by frequenting society, gained in prestige; they had learned the manners of the world and things they could not have gleaned in books. What this means is that writers owed their positive image to their place in social circles, to their growing worldliness. In short, they had learned to leave the library for the salon, bypassing Parnassus, possibly avoiding Grub Street, and thereby creating a new literary space.

Duclos makes several distinctions among men of letters bearing upon the changes which have occurred. There are savants and scholars, types which were formerly held in high esteem. The Renaissance was essentially their work, but they have fallen into disfavor and their numbers are diminishing. This is unfortunate, for the profession of letters stands to profit from knowledge. They do not frequent the world much, finding it not to their liking, a feeling reciprocated by society. A second distinction is that of the learned men who occupy themselves with the exact sciences. Such men are respected, their names known, and their utility recognized, and they are

*132*

sometimes rewarded for their services. But their names are more likely to be fashionable in certain circles than their persons, unless they also happened to possess social graces more prized by the world than their science. Duclos's distinction between these first two types is important, for he effectively separates the scholars of the humanistic tradition from the men engaged in the natural sciences, physics, and mathematics. It is a distinction not as sharply drawn in the various literary histories and lives of the period.

The third category of writers Duclos distinguished were the *beaux-esprits*. They are the ones most sought after by society. But again he makes a further distinction, between those who acquire success in their art but can also show talent and a variety of imagination which goes beyond it, and those whose talent is limited to their art. A case in point may have been Corneille, a great tragic poet but very poor company, whereas Voltaire excelled both in letters and in society. The world sought the man of wit within the successful writer, poet, artist. But more is implied in this distinction, for Duclos also discerned the new social role of wit, which is distinct from talent. "Men of talent must have more fame, that is their recompense. Persons of wit must find more pleasure in society, since they bring more to it; it is a well-founded recognition" (*Considérations*, p. 215). His remark points to a phenomenon linked to literature. Fréron had also remarked that men of letters had become men of the world, fops, and successful with women. Wit could advance the man of letters who wrote mere trifles or frequented the right circles, producing now and then a poem or a discourse submitted for an academic prize, and with such light baggage entered the Academy. Chamfort's career before 1789 comes readily to mind, and indeed it can be said that his *Maximes et anecdotes,* published after his death, are a literary testament to or product of this new role of wit. It had become literature, an art of conversation exercised within that new literary space which finds its centers not in libraries but salons. The great resource of the writer was, in part at least, his capacity to amuse the bored of the upper classes. Wit enlivened society, and it was precisely in

*133*

the meeting of such wits and society that both the new status of the writer and a new literary space, one reserved to the play of intelligence, repartee, and the formation of public opinion, were created. Rousseau was aware of this, for he was painfully unable to play the wit, but since society would accept almost any role less boring than the traditional ones, even being gruff and antisocial came to be accepted from the writer. Furthermore, Duclos observed that the writer gained a certain equality. "It is said gambling and love equalize conditions among men: I am convinced wit would have been added if the proverb had been devised since wit has become a passion. Gambling equalizes by lowering the superior, love by raising the inferior, and wit because true equality is of the soul" (*Considérations*, p. 216). This too is a radical change from the literary space of the library, where liberty reigned, but where nothing was said of social equality.

Duclos also recognized the changed condition and role of men of letters in the power accorded public opinion, precisely the province of the man of letters. "The powerful command and men of wit govern, because in the end they form public opinion, which sooner or later subjugates or overcomes all forms of despotism" (p. 217). Public opinion, however, was not the work of men of letters alone, but of the wit produced by the polish, ease, and requirement not to be tedious demanded of the writer in the fashionable world. The new elite of the eighteenth century was composed of individuals of various fixed social strata or conditions, or, if you will, social orders, to use a term sometimes associated with the society of the Old Régime. Duclos poses an aristocracy of the mind and recommends a politics for the writer as wit: he ought to prefer the court to lesser social ranks because men and women of the nobility are beyond vanity. "The higher one is, the less one tends to stress a distance too marked to be missed" (p. 218). The writer is also likely to find good protection there. Yet he also issues a warning: do not try to penetrate that world, let yourself be invited. "You belong to society by birth and dignities; you attach yourself to it for reasons of interest; you may insinuate yourself into it by way of base acts, or may be linked to it by alliances with persons of fortune; you may be admitted by choice, this being the lot of men of letters; and relations based on taste necessarily make for distinctions" (p. 220).

The social success of a few writers was not without drawbacks. Letters were perceived as a possible avenue of social success, but a great many untalented writers would have been better off never entering the Republic of Letters. Although failing to advance, they later found that they were incapable of doing anything else but writing. Thus the social success of the few, the arrival of a handful on the heights of the Parnassus now perceived to be the Académie française, did not preclude the continued existence of Grub Street. Below Parnassus were literary failures, a literary proletariat, and various enemies of literature in a bohemia without romance. Furthermore, success creates envy, and offers merely the pleasures of society. But the worst enemies of literature and writers were fools, *les sots:* they represent men of letters as dangerous, ambitious intriguers, and do not suppose that it is possible to use one's wits in a manner different from theirs. This is erroneous: men of letters are not dangerous to society, but rather are dedicated to study, the sciences, and letters. They are incapable of intrigues, and the love of letters is such that it leaves its devotees indifferent to cupidity and ambition. They may well be better than most men; for instance, look at their loyalty to Fouquet after his disgrace. "La Fontaine, Pelisson, and Mademoiselle de Scudéry went so far as to expose themselves to the king's resentment, and even to that of his ministers" (p. 220). Duclos is linking *esprit* to *vertu,* and thereby altering the image of the man of letters, preparing that of the writer as philosophe. In the same vein he pleads for unity among men of letters, and with this call for unity of mind and purpose, and peace in the Republic of Letters, the man of letters had acquired full consciousness of himself. But the best treatise on the man of letters in history and society was not written by Duclos, Diderot, d'Alembert, Mercier, or La Harpe, but by a rather obscure professor of the Collège de France.

Jean-Jacques Garnier's *L'Homme de lettres* (1764) is, like

Duclos's chapter on the man of letters, concerned with definitions of this new type become a common figure in society. But his work is a more serious undertaking than the essays and epistles of the various members of the Academy who sang their own praises or the poems of contestants for prizes in poetry or eloquence; it is also quite different from the first of such treatises, Father Daniello Bartoli's *Dell' Huomo di lettere* (Venice, 1648; republished in a translation by Father de Livoy in 1768). The man of letters one met in the salons of Parisian society, at the Procope, or in the course of the public meetings of the Academy bore no resemblance to Bartoli's retiring and introspective writer.

Garnier was well aware of the novel character of the man of letters in the eighteenth century, for even the term *l'homme de lettres* had not existed earlier. Antiquity preferred to use words such as *philosopher, poet, orator,* or *sophist,* and the Roman word *litterator* referred to what in Garnier's day was called a *demi-savant.* He found the origin of the man of letters in the modern sense in the sixteenth century, with the invention and development of printing. Garnier, without explicitly saying so, ties him to the book. The term was extended to and confused with the learned, the scholars who knew a great deal and yet were not philosophers, poets, or orators. Rather, they had made study their principal occupation in life, and *homme de lettres* came to be as vague as *homme d'épée* or *homme de robe.* In the eighteenth century, Garnier thought, the term was so vague as to be almost impossible to define. The populace confused the man of letters with an author, and fashionable society thought of him as an amusing person who spoke well in receptions and social circles. Even writers did not know what it meant because they tended to restrict the term to those in their own branch of learning and because men of letters had neglected to study their own past. Garnier, as the works of Jean-Pierre Nicéron and Claude Pierre Gouget demonstrate, was not quite right here, but his was nevertheless the first attempt to write a systematic treatise on men of letters as a class rather than a compilation of lives and a bibliography of works.

Garnier based his definition on a contrast with the artist or architect. Whereas the painter imitates objects by means of color to acquire a fortune and reputation, the man of letters's principal task was to cultivate his mind through study "in order to render himself better and more useful to society" (*L'Homme de lettres,* p. 7). There is no mention of writing a book, for the man of letters is not necessarily an author. Garnier's definition has brought us beyond La Bruyère's "métier de faire un livre." The sciences and the arts which affect the soul and mind of man were the province of the man of letters, for their aim is not gain so much as the disinterested pursuit of truth and useful knowledge. This question of gain is important to Garnier, as it was to be to Rousseau, and he stresses that Socrates, concerned with the same problem, confused the sophist who taught for gain with the sophist as philosopher. The distinction, Garnier argues, must be maintained, for the point is whether one exercises the profession for money or for its own sake. "He who would but propose to sell at high price a lesson in rhetoric would only be a merchant of words" (p. 9).

The man of letters's prime occupation must be study. Thus while Augustus and Hadrian were *princes lettrés,* government took too much of their time for them to be men of letters, unlike Marcus Aurelius and Julian, who were men of letters first and emperors second. "The man of letters, no matter his rank, is principally occupied with bettering his soul: he works on himself and is both the block of marble and the sculptor" (p. 12). Garnier's model or archetypal man of letters was Socrates, the master of dialectic, the art of posing and answering questions. But even if Garnier's man of letters is a philosopher, it is doubtful that he is a philosophe or that Garnier thought of Diderot when he used Socrates as a model. Yet there are similarities between Diderot's view of himself and Garnier's discussion of dialectics, if only because Diderot was ready to talk about anything.

Garnier's discussion of dialectics as a master art in a sense rivals d'Alembert's organization of knowledge as well as his view of the philosophe. D'Alembert's ideal of the philosophe is based on modern knowledge; Garnier's moral image of the man of letters is based on Plato. He is to have a "certain elevation of soul which makes him look with disdain on riches and honors and everything else which does not contribute to the enlightenment and virtue of mankind" (p. 64). This does sound somewhat like Diderot's Moi in his dialectic with Rameau-Lui, but Garnier's book is not really an exposition of the man of letters as Diderot may have thought of him. Rather, his treatise turns into something unlike earlier essays on men of letters; it becomes a treatise on education which insists upon the value of *un maître,* a master in the classical sense, a mature man with disciples. If Mercier and Doigny Du Ponceau's lyrical view of the man of letters evokes the sentimental genre pictures of Greuze, Garnier's reminds one of David's *Socrates.* Even his recommended reading is based on his love of antiquity; he creates an image of the antique sage in a modern setting, fully aware of the obstacles inherent in modern society to the cultivation of mind and soul. Here it is not so much Diderot that comes to mind as Rousseau, for to Garnier, as for Rousseau, solitude was essential to the man of letters. If the preference for isolation were lost, the writer would soon turn into a man of the world writing amusing trifles or vulgarizations. This skeptical view of the effects of social intercourse does not apply to the society of other men of letters, which may be a fruitful stimulus to thought. And while Garnier praised solitude, he does not preclude the need for a library. "For men and women of the world, a library is a piece of furniture; for men of letters it is a tool" (p. 111).

But, Garnier wonders, if letters were a noble calling, why was the profession so often ridiculed? The question testifies to the persistence of a negative image of writers in spite of the philosophes' reevaluation of the social role of letters. The best men did not always enter into letters so that the profession filled with lesser minds. And in a society such as that of the French monarchy, in which rank was determined by birth, the man of letters was an exile within the state, procuring neither brilliant honors nor distinguished positions. Proud, independent, and courageous souls shunned such obscurity. Only low birth or a modest fortune could keep even those born to letters by temperament and inclination in that career. There were those who chose the profession as a living, persisted in seeking the light of truth, and, having become authors after a hard struggle, found themselves objects of ridicule in society. Most of these perished in obscurity. Or there were gentle characters who were carried to letters by inertia; study became their way of life, books their love, and their patronage the benefit of the Republic of Letters. But there were also those who became writers in order to seek a reputation and climb the social scale.

Nevertheless, in spite of what the world thought of letters as a career, and however it judged men of letters, there could be no doubt letters were useful to the state and society. Garnier assigned to letters an important historical, moral, civilizing role, and in this he was at one with the philosophes. The ancients knew the value of education well enough to make it a concern of the state. But men of letters were of value in another sense. They lent a nation prestige vis-à-vis its neighbors, which is a better type of rivalry than that of arms. Its effects last longer, and culture becomes a force which draws people to one's capital and makes for admiration and respect. It stood to reason, therefore, that the state ought to compensate writers for their services by way of distinctions, offices, employment, and consideration. These flatter men of letters and provoke emulation. But rewards should not be in the form of money because the writer must ever beware of the attractions of luxury, ease, and wealth. Garnier disapproved of pensions, which he distinguished from offices. In appointing a writer to an office the state received service in return, but giving a pension isolated him, forced him upon himself, and in effect reduced him to a state of dependency. An office made use of a man in recognition of his worth; a pension made a beggar of him.

On the whole, Garnier thought, it was better to be poor, for even experienced in a state of poverty close to indigence, the life of letters was not without attractions. The man of letters avoided the three main sources of human ills: ignorance, passions, and boredom. He preferred friendship to love,

139

and he should marry, if at all, only a kindred vigorous soul, another Hypatia—should he be lucky enough to meet one. The writer's true offspring were his books, and these ought to be the only ones required of him. Garnier had better judgment than to sing the praises of motherhood, fatherhood, and an increasing population. He considered "the cares and encumbrances of a household . . . ill suited to the calm and indifference necessary to the exercise of the mind" (p. 192). Far better study, which elevates the mind and soul beyond the vices of avarice and cupidity, and far better the cultivation of that imagination which allows one to follow Plato to the Academy, to walk with delight in the garden of Epicurus, and to love virtue in the commerce of the Stoa.

Garnier's *L'Homme de lettres* is an important work in the history of the consciousness men of letters and intellectuals came to have of themselves and their profession. Certain features associated with the space of the library survived in the book, but the poets did not fare very well, and there is nothing of Parnassus in it, not even the metaphor. But there are also affinities between his view of men of letters and that of the philosophes, in that both insisted upon the social and moral role of the man of letters in history. Garnier also points to some of the issues of the time, such as the question raised by the effect of money and the *beau monde* on the writer's vocation. And unlike other treatises, his work contains a historical outline of the genealogy of men of letters. Garnier first finds them among the Egyptian priests, then the magi, and later among the Greek poets and other types produced by the Greeks, such as philosophers, legislators, and orators, finally ending with considerations on men of letters among the Romans. The conscious image of the man of letters therefore seemed complete by the 1760s, but one aspect remained to be treated. It might be considered another facet of the negative image, for it concerns the sickness of men of letters.

Dr. Samuel A. A. D. Tissot's *De la santé des gens de lettres* (1768) must surely be counted as a portrait of the man of letters, even if it is presented from an entirely different perspective than that usually chosen. In a sense Tissot's book belongs to the earlier years of the eighteenth century, for the diseases he described are more those of men of letters of that period than of the more mundane Parisian writers frequenting the salons. Be that as it may, the work did not appear until after the man of letters had been singled out as a social type, and Tissot's book is an interesting piece of medical sociology. It is most suggestive in that it includes what other images of the man of letters left out. Men of letters belonged to certain literary spaces; Tissot's contribution was to give them a bodily position which in part explains their diseases. "The diseases of men of letters have two principal sources: the hard work of the mind and the continuous repose of the body; to make an exact tableau of these one need but trace in detail the nefarious effects of these two causes" (p. 15). Not only were writers poor, but they were liable to sicknesses directly connected with their work. The image of the writer is sharpened to the point that his work and thought is made visible in his physiognomy. The meditating man has facial muscles so tense that he appears to be in convulsions. Thinking fatigues not only the brain but the entire body, and reading makes for other bad side effects. "The inconveniences of frivolous books are a waste of time and tired eyesight; but those who by the power and liaison of ideas lift the soul beyond itself and force it to meditate wear out the spirit and exhaust the body, and the greater and longer this pleasure, the more fatal the results" (pp. 19–20). Tissot mentions several cases to support his opinion: one writer's arm swelled when he experienced a lively sensation or thought; another completely ruined his mind with mathematics; and several showed signs of anxiety. Metaphysics especially caused some individuals extreme fatigue and stupor. The effects on the stomach are also bad. "The man who thinks the most is the man who has the worst digestion, all things being equal; he who thinks the least, has the best digestion" (p. 25)—a maxim which ought to create suspicion of healthy-looking professors, writers, and other intellectuals. He quotes a Portuguese doctor who opined that a poor stomach followed men of letters as the shadow follows the body, and cites Boerhaave, who thought study ruined the stomach, which could lead to melancholia. The effects of these nervous disorders are general lassitude, pusillanimity, sadness, discouragement, fear, hypochondria, weak nerves, and other diseases. Of course the profession of letters also made for pale complexions, consumption, thin bodies, and frequent heart flutters.

Tissot went on to catalogue even worse effects, such as various forms of hallucination or even fits of madness, which are due to the incapacity of the soul to control the brain. For example, Pascal always thought he was on the edge of a pit of fire; Barloeus thought his mind was made of butter and always avoided heat for fear of melting; and Jurieu attributed his colic to seven horsemen fighting each other in his entrails. Men of letters are also frequently given to headaches, insomnia, and eventually apoplexy, a very common cause of death among them. Savants or scholars are most prone to these diseases, for they tend to avoid ordinary human intercourse in order to concentrate entirely on their passion for erudition, medals, inscriptions, rare books, and manuscripts. Generally they are far too sedentary, which frequently causes dropsy and sicknesses connected with the lower organs. Hypochondria also results from this type of life. Reading during meals hurts digestion, and an excess of work makes for retention of urine and difficulties in evacuating solids.

This is a sad image indeed of the man of letters, and far from the images of glory connected with Parnassus, Apollo, and the Muses. In Tissot's view, the new idea of creativity in solitude, the image of the genius contained in contemporary writings, is not to be recommended. In solitude too he sees a cause of disease, for it creates languor and even worse.

> Nothing contributes more to health than the joys of social intercourse which are stifled by solitude, and this moral cause of ennui, joined to the physical causes of melancholia, . . . often plunges men of letters into a mournful state whose effects on health are as nefarious as a cheerful state is beneficial; it is this which produces that melancholy, chagrined spirit, discontent,

*142*

and general disgust which may be regarded as among the greatest evils, since it spoils the enjoyment of everything.

[P. 96]

Given this opinion, romanticism as a disease seems more than a metaphor.

Tissot, however, also held forth hope, for he proposed certain remedies or preventive measures. The most difficult thing, he felt, was to get the men of letters to change their habits. They are very stubborn indeed and suffer from the fixity of ideas which comes from study and is augmented by the good opinion they have of themselves. What is needed for good health is not to overwork. The mind needs relaxation, distraction, or distension. Scholars would do well to leave their studies now and then to walk, renew themselves, and exercise their bodies. They should also be careful as to what they eat, avoiding fattening foods, meats hardened by salting and smoking, and sour foods. Instead they ought to concentrate on young, tender meat, eat cereals of various sorts in soups or broths, grasses like chicory, bread, eggs, milk, chocolate, and fruits. Not more than three dishes ought to be served per meal, and men of letters would also be well advised not to eat too often; two light meals or one substantial one will suffice, and they should not eat a heavy meal before bed. Water ought to be preferred to wine, for the latter is not good for men of letters because it moves the humors to the brain, which is already exposed to the ills common to them. It should only be used as a remedy, especially for fatigue, weakness, and depression. Tea, coffee, and tobacco are bad too. Finally, let men of letters live in good air, avoid extreme climates, and since most live in cities, choose a good, airy, and well-lighted apartment, with a chimney rather than an oven because of their propensity to cold feet.

Tissot's work is interesting for what it tells indirectly about men of letters. If their poor humor, vanity, and irascible character was in Baillet's time explained as an effect of man's sinful nature, Tissot explains it in terms of the new philosophy of nature applied to medicine. For Linguet literature was a social disease; for Tissot men of letters were prone to certain sicknesses. The romantic disease denounced by Linguet is diagnosed as a form of melancholia by Tissot. But the doctor's prescription for good health among men of letters, while sound, could hardly be expected to be widely applied. The majority of Grub Street writers probably could not afford young, tender meat, airy apartments, and the rest of his recommendations. And surely wine was a consolation for an ungrateful existence when one could afford it. Perhaps the healthy man of letters was as much an ideal as the philosophe as envisaged by Diderot or, for that matter, Garnier.

The revised image of the man of letters did not erase the old negative image, but it did transform it. In the age of Baillet, it was the critic as then understood—as scholar, as pedant—who seems to be the resumé of all the faults of the literary type, and in fact Baillet has little good to say about men of letters. The emphasis is on liberty and its consequences, disagreements of various sorts, prejudices, and the variability of opinion concerning books in the Republic of Letters. There is no reference made to any extra literary space. But the revised image of the eighteenth-century man of letters in effect created two different classes of writers: the respectable and the less respectable, or, to put it more succinctly, the arrived and the failures. The first group tended in the second half of the century to call themselves philosophes, while the second was composed of those who were looked upon with disdain by the successful, were in pronounced and open opposition to the philosophic party, and were sometimes associated with specific critics, such as Fréron and, later, Sabatier de Castres. Garnier's man of letters is an ideal type of which it is difficult to find examples on the historical level. One does think of Diderot, whose ideal was similar, but Diderot was a partisan of a cause, while Garnier's man of letters cannot be associated with one. Literary space had become political in the 1760s. This new space was more multifaceted than the space of the library, limited to literary scholars and a few poets. The literary man had changed. Instead of restricting himself to the library or aiming for the alternative heights of Parnassus, he now dared to measure himself against the ruling circles. Baillet had insisted on liberty within the Republic of Letters, but his discussion or insistence was quite separate from any social considerations and conducted as if the ruling circles did not read. His argument implied that the liberty of the Republic of Letters was limited only by the potential for critical freedom, and, at the other extreme, the accepted truths of religion (which did not seem to bother scholars very much). But what preoccupied the new man of letters of the eighteenth century, the philosophe as well as others, was precisely the question of independence.

Given the new conditions of literature, including its fashionableness and the market aspect of an expanded Grub Street, the question of money was bound to be posed as it never had been before. The negative image of the writer changed because it was now only the poor, unsuccessful, ill-paid writer who cut a poor figure, rather than the writer as such. Within the literary space of the library the man of letters had been free in part because material conditions were not his primary concern, because that space was not coextensive with Grub Street, and because scholars had either private incomes, protection, livings, remunerations from the owners of libraries in which they served as librarians, salaries as tutors, income as members of the church. Poets were another matter, for it ought to be underlined that the negative image of the man of letters in the seventeenth century was that of the penniless poet or the ridiculous pedant. Between these extremes there were a great many scholars born into the robe who were neither poor nor ridiculous. Also, the liberty of the Republic of Letters was psychological and mental; it hardly referred to social conditions, politics, or established power, and was generally restricted to those who made up the republic itself. But with the expansion of literary space, literary men came into contact with the *grand monde* and the *beau monde,* as well as the marketplace, raising the issue of the writer's independence. Could he remain free within this new literary space? This question was in fact related to another: Was writing to be a profession like any other in which one worked for money, or was it to remain a disinterested and therefore noble activity?

It is significant that Garnier posed this very question, distinguishing between the sophist and the philosopher on this basis. But he was not alone in this preoccupation, for the noble disinterestedness of the writer seemed to leave him poor but make the publisher rich. Publishers had no scruples about making money and did not ask themselves about the uses of literature. For them, as Rémond de Saint-Sauveur pointed out, a book was a product to be sold, and forbidden books seemed even more marketable than approved ones. Thus the literary space of the library, coextensive with liberty of mind and the disinterested pursuit of knowledge (however altered by the foibles of a corrupt human nature), came into conflict with the literary marketplace. The *métier de faire un livre,* still in its handcraft stage when La Bruyère wrote the phrase, had by the middle of the eighteenth century turned into a veritable capitalist enterprise.

Both Voltaire and Desfontaines, one recalls (and one ought not be surprised if Voltaire got the idea from the critic), defended the production of bad novels on the grounds that such works employed a great many people. Indeed, from this point of view, writing for publication may well serve as the archetypal model of the capitalist entrepreneurial system: mind is capital, writing is work, producing the book is division of labor, and the book itself is a product which can be bought and sold. But in the eighteenth century this investment by writing seemed on the whole to work only in favor of the publishers.

Georges Fenouillot de Falbaire, in a pamphlet entitled *Avis aux gens de lettres* (1770), revealed those aspects of the history of literature which for so long have escaped the notice of historians of literature who write in terms of the conflict of ideas, the evolution of genres, or the critical assessment of well-established works. Fenouillot's point is that ever since the invention of printing publishers have almost alone gathered the fruits borne by writers. He argued that they were even persuaded that they were the masters of literature, and they took to court writers who disputed their assumed rights. The pamphlet discusses the case of Luneau de Boisjermain, an author who published and distributed his own works rather than pass through the officially recognized corporation of booksellers. In other words, the questions of money and literary property were becoming a prime concern precisely at the time the image of the man of letters had been revised, and Fenouillot was telling writers that they had been fools, and that literary glory was but a sham which had kept writers starving for centuries. As he puts it, the book-sellers "are quite willing not to contest an author *his literary superiority*. So long as he leaves them his purse, they gladly leave him his laurels" (p. 14). The booksellers-publishers had come to think that putting writers to work, producing books, and selling them for a profit was the essential part of their trade and entirely their affair and monopoly. They thought wholly in terms of business: they manufactured books like stockings and hats. The writers, thanks to their revised view of themselves, thought otherwise. If the man of letters and his work was useful to the nation and enlightened mankind, by comparison the bookseller was but a boor. The old distinction between the noble and the merchant was thus transferred into the new literary space, as the activity of writing became the mere production of merchandise. Fenouillot de Falbaire referred to book jobbers as *courtiers ingrats* and insolent subalterns; the writer is the superior man who in effect nourishes them. The writer has a sacred natural right to his property, his work. It is writers who spread abroad a language and a nation's reputation; it was French writers who made of French a universal language, and yet this very class of citizens is ill treated at home and expected to work for practically nothing at a time when literature is all the rage in a society resting on money: "The greater part of great lords spend their life in courts crawling, flattering, intriguing to obtain favors, which, as a final result, are always money" (p. 33). To be sure the writer has few needs, finds his joy in the world of the imagination, and never entered letters to accumulate wealth, but the soldier, cleric, or clerk may hope to rise to riches, and only the writer has an unpromising future. "He alone discovers before him only an arid and sterile terrain in which work does not suffice to keep misery at bay;

147

only he can be filled with triumphs without finding his subsistence, and at the end only die in the midst of glory and poverty" (p. 35). Fenouillot's description shows acutely that the revised image had in no way affected the poverty of the actual writer in general. The glory is granted, the penniless poet and the ridiculous pedant are no longer the issue, and letters have become a profession, but a profession in which one is not to be paid. The complaint comes at the time when publishers were rich and the nobility was no longer believed in. The new literary space was that of capitalism, and in this new space the writer belonged to the exploited poor. "Almost all men of letters are born poor: for the poor man, possessing but his soul, is, so to say, forced to cultivate the only good nature gave him" (p. 36). The rich man is liable to dissipate himself and his soul. But whereas an ordinary artisan can live off his work, the writer cannot, because "publishers here swallow all the profit produced by the books published. And thus they have gained quick and prodigious fortunes which ought to surprise no one. A man who had nothing when starting out in business will find himself after ten or fifteen years with a fortune of seven or eight hundred thousand francs" (p. 38). Michelot, Fenouillot says, earned 100,000 francs from the *Caractères* of La Bruyère, to whom he gave 100 écus for the manuscript. The English writer is far better off, as witness Robertson, who received 4,000 guineas for his *History of Charles V.* In France, on the other hand, the publishers of the *Encyclopédie* made 2,000,000 livres, while Diderot the editor slaved away at about 2,500 livres per year and an annuity of 100 pistoles.

Indeed, the *Encyclopédie,* usually lauded in modern literary histories as par excellence a monument of enlightenment, weapon against superstition, and milestone on the road towards liberty, equality, and fraternity is also one of the foremost capitalist enterprises of the eighteenth century. From the five volumes of text and one of engravings planned in 1745, it grew to attain, over twenty-five years, seventeen volumes of print and eleven of engravings, to employ over 150 collaborators and meet the demands of 4,000 subscribers. Voltaire thought that over 1,000 paper makers, printers, binders, and engravers lived from it, and that a capital of 7,650,000 livres had been put into circulation by this publishing venture.

Viewed from this perspective, the *Encyclopédie* is certainly a turning point in the history of letters, but perhaps more in terms of literary production than of the history of ideas. The individual art of writing and the disinterested labor of the scholar were organized into a collective enterprise and capitalist venture based on the industrial principle of division of labor. The man of letters may have thought of himself as a gentleman and a culturally useful man of mind when he was in the salons of the well-to-do and the great, and he was probably sure of his superiority when he was a member of the Académie française, but when he worked for the publisher Le Breton, or, later on, Panckoucke, he was an employee. "Diderot," writes Jacques Proust, "is the very type of the writer torn between his function as an artist and his condition as a man, between the imperatives of his thought and art and those of a society in which gold is king" (*Diderot et l'Encyclopédie*, p. 115). Diderot did rise above Grub Street, but not to riches. At the end of his life he enjoyed, at best, the modest comfort and security of the *petit bourgeois*. He was not as poor as Lenglet Du Fresnoy nor even Rousseau, but measured against the fortunes of those for whom he had worked, his reward for a long life of literary slavery was meager. Yet he was among those for whom writing was a profession, and he accepted the capitalist view of literary work as against the "noble" view.

It is possible to discern within the new literary space of the new elite, created by the philosophes as well as by the new market situation, three paths open to the writer. Diderot may be regarded as representing one new view, that of writing as a profession in which the writer lives off his writing, however little he may earn, and in which he accepts the capitalist view of literary labor. Diderot preferred freedom based on a contract to protection or other earlier forms of patronage. The second possibility was also new and may have resulted from writers' unwillingness to accept the market. It is perhaps best exemplified by Rousseau, and is writing as a vocation, irrespective of the risks; writing is not seen as a career. Finally, there is a transformed survival of the noble view of writing as a disinterested gentleman's pursuit of truth, knowledge, and, in the case of belles lettres, perfection and form. This is represented by d'Alembert, and is the academic view of writing, which transforms the man of letters into a member of a new lettered and thinking elite which differs both from the professional writer and from the man who feels he *must* write because he has something to say. With this third view, the writer is assimilated to the régime and is on his way to becoming a notable.

The link between Diderot's acceptance of the conditions of literary life within the new literary space of his time and the old Grub Street is obvious, and d'Alembert's elitist view of the life of letters can also be traced back to the Republic of Letters and the space of the library. But Rousseau's attitude is unprecedented, and since he had begun like so many others who aspired to glory on Parnassus, it is worth looking at his life in letters in greater detail. When Rousseau first arrived in Paris in 1741, he was rather well connected, thanks to the abbé de Mably whom he had met in Lyon. But, as he admitted, this initial advantage did not lead him very far. His musical notation system failed to earn him the glory he had hoped for, and yet he persisted in working on it because he realized that celebrity in the arts meant a fortune in Paris. Thus he acted like many others come from the provinces or foreign parts to make a start in the capital: get its attention, and then rise to fortune, fame, and glory. He published his scheme, paid the privilège for it, and got nothing in return but a review. Eventually he even stopped seeing the very people who might have advanced him, and only kept his acquaintance with Marivaux, Mably, Fontenelle, and Diderot. Throughout his early years in Paris then, Rousseau lived at a level even below that of the much despised journalists who were supporting themselves by writing. Rousseau did nothing; he read poetry and spent what money he had left. Father Castel, a Jesuit of his acquaintance who was interested in a new scheme of musical notation based on color, pointed to another expedient for success in Paris. He advised Rousseau to try women, and introduced him to those with influence, among them Madame de Beuzenval, spouse of the colonel of the Swiss Guard, through whom he met Madame de Broglie and Madame Dupin.

It was at Madame de Beuzenval's that Rousseau was invited to dinner and was flattered until he found he was to eat with the servants. He comments: "She had little idea of the respects owed talents" (*Confessions,* p. 289). In truth Rousseau expected too much for the 1740s, but it is undeniable that by the time he was writing his *Confessions* talents were the fashion and writers were no longer confused with domestic servants, and he may have been judging this early action precisely in terms of this later development. In any case Madame de Broglie saved the situation at the time by inviting him to dine with her and President de Lamoignon and Rousseau, for his part, saved himself from ridicule by a judicious silence during dinner. Afterwards he compensated for his lack of social graces by reading the company a verse epistle on his misfortunes. Madame de Broglie gave him a copy of Duclos's *Confessions du comte de* ———— , a novel by a well-connected writer whom Rousseau soon met and liked.

With Madame Dupin he was received into a famous salon and the milieu of money, the great, men of letters, and beautiful women, all of which ought to have helped him greatly. As it happened, his connections did not produce an entry into letters but rather into the diplomatic service, which he soon gave up to return to Paris and a second début. This time, however, Rousseau began to look differently upon society: he would, he later wrote, be independent, and he resumed work on an opera he had begun in Venice. He was also introduced to La Popelinière, a great patron of music. Although this second musical début also did not succeed, he found employment doing research for Dupin de Francueil, thereby making 900 francs a year for himself and Thérèse and her family. It was subsistence living, dependence on the rich at whose tables he ate. He also made contact with another family of financiers, that of Madame d'Epinay, kept up his friendship with Diderot and Condillac, and learned something about publishers. "The Paris publishers are arrogant and hard for all beginners" (*Confessions,* p. 347).

Rousseau never did achieve fame in music; his triumph came instead in letters, nine years after his first stay in Paris. He has some rather revealing things to say in his *Confessions* about the condition of the man of letters, a condition he knew well from his own experience as well as from the milieu he had frequented for many years before he withdrew into his solitude. He earned his income by copying music because he did not wish to write for money. Thus even Rousseau proposed an image of the writer as a philosophe, but his philosophe was probably closer to Garnier's than to d'Alembert's. In any case, writing ought to be nonvenal.

> No, no, I have always felt that the writer's estate could be respectable and illustrious only insofar as it was not a job. It is too difficult to think nobly when one thinks only in order to live. To dare and be able to say great truths one must not depend upon success. I sent my books among the public convinced of having spoken for the common good without care for the rest. If the work was rebuked, so much the worse for those who would not profit from it.
>
> [P. 403]

It is an interesting passage because of the context: letters were a career, letters were a profit-making enterprise, and Rousseau distinguishes between that and the position of the illustrious author. The new division within the Republic of Letters is explicit here, and Rousseau expounds a noble view which is closer to the space of the library than to the new marketplace. But there has been a notable change of attitude. Baillet, were he to rewrite the last sentence, would surely have said that if the work were refused by the public, so much the worse for the author. The shift of emphasis is striking: the readers and critics of the old Republic of Letters, the writer's risks upon publication, have been displaced by a view of the writer as important to society and sure of his calling. The public had changed: it was far wider than that of the literary space of the library and it seemed more passive. The whole phenomenon of writers, books, and reputations had changed radically since the early eighteenth century.

But despite his noble views, Rousseau continued to frequent the houses of the rich, and he was not the independent man he wished to be. He too lived the contradictions of the man of letters at this time, as much as if not more than Diderot. But if Diderot's compensatory image of the man of letters was that of his visits and dinners in Granval, Rousseau's concept of the independent man of letters was completed by a different image, a picturesque image of the writer in his small country house. The Hermitage defines a literary space at the opposite pole from the marketplace. It was not really new, for such a retreat had been the dream of the humanist scholar, as well as of the poets of the seventeenth century, but it had significant implications in Rousseau's time because of its separation from the market. Rousseau at the Hermitage fulfills a writer's dream: he had peace, tranquillity, and meditation in nature. It is an archetypal image of the hermit and sage on the profane level. The image stuck; Mercier in his vision of a future Paris envisages the Académie française transferred to the heights of Montmartre, with its members living in separate little cottages. And Ledoux, in his plans for an ideal city, did not fail to design a house for a man of letters which guarantees the silence, solitude, and privacy necessary to create the great thoughts needed by society. Rousseau, however, still was not free in the Hermitage. It did not belong to him, and he could not avoid society.

> I had an isolated dwelling in a charming solitude; my own master, I could do there as I wished without control from anyone; but this habitation imposed certain duties, easily filled, but indispensable. My entire liberty was only precarious; more subdued than if under orders, I was mastered by my will: there was not a day on which I could rise and say to myself I would spend it as I pleased. More, besides my dependence upon Madame d'Epinay's plans, I had another more importunate one from the public and passers-by. The distance from Paris was not such as to prevent daily arrivals of the idle, who, not knowing what to do with their time, spent mine without any scruple.

> [*Confessions*, p. 425]

The fashion for letters had at last caught up with the writer, who had come far from the days when he was looked upon as a ridiculous figure in society. But being an object of interest had distinct disadvantages. The writer had become a spectacle, a new type of father confessor, a saint to be called on, or an *amuseur* good for a supper party, all of which roles were in fact dangers to what drove writers in the first place, the inner necessity to write. The intimate space of the writer described by Maurice Blanchot was imperiled by the very success of literature. In the eighteenth century apologists of writing such as Garnier would have put it differently: the world pressed in upon the writer and left him no time to dream, no time for the pleasures of his imagination. Letters as a career threatened this intimate interior space.

Rousseau at one time was offered a position on the *Journal des savants* which consisted of writing two reviews per month, and it would have meant, as he admitted, entering a society of men of great merit, like Dortous de Mairan, Alexis Clairaut, Joseph de Guignes, and the abbé Barthelemy, and also would have meant a little money. But Rousseau refused even this none too arduous task. "I knew that my talent came only from a certain warmth of the soul concerning the subject I had to treat, and that only the love of the great, the true, and the beautiful could animate my genius, while the subjects I should have had to extract, and most of the books themselves, would have been nothing to me" (*Confessions,* p. 513). The distinction made between careerists and the noble calling of letters carries over into the very act of writing. Grub Street is the space of writers who can and will write on anything, but in Rousseau's own literary space of intimacy, an interior space so to say, such prostitution is no longer possible. Ultimately, his attitude is based on his fundamental distinction between nature and society. Grub Street is society, but the act of writing from conviction and passion is the voice of nature. The true writer is a prophet. Rousseau is important in that he reflects on the very act of writing: he has shifted the old "métier de faire un livre" onto another level of consciousness. La Bruyère said that not anyone can write a book because it is not just thoughts put down on paper by someone who happens to possess knowledge or wit; a book is constructed, something separate from thinking and writing. But Rousseau argues that the craft is far less important than what is said. He had perceived that the book had become a commercial item, that one's thoughts could be sold, and that writing was a kind of alienation. Writing, an artistic problem in the time of La Bruyère, had become a moral problem, and Rousseau "considered quitting literature altogether, and above all the job of writing" (p. 513). He thought of this not so much because writing was alienating, for his recognition of that is implied more than formulated in his works, but because he had come to dislike the literary milieu and seen how expensive it had become for him to be famous. "If I dined in town at some distance from home, rather than letting me take a cab, the lady of the house insisted on harnessing her coach to send me back; she was glad to spare me twenty-four sous but never thought of the escudo I gave her coachman" (pp. 514–15). Obviously Rousseau is describing a fashionable marginality which turned out to be expensive not only in the time it took from one's writing, but also financially. For while his writing sold rather well, it did not make him at all rich. In addition to the Hermitage, Rousseau had another marvelous retreat at the Petit Château de Montmorency, then belonging to the maréchal de Luxembourg. But again, while he moved in high circles, his imagination got the better of him and he became too familiar, while the Luxembourgs always knew how to keep their distance. Rousseau exemplifies the problem of the intelligent writer in the world of high society in which manners are not the result of intelligence or knowledge, but of convention. Voltaire, who had grown up in such circles, never had to face that problem.

Part of Rousseau's significance, shared with other philosophes, lies in that the man of letters, formerly defined with reference to the library, the temple, or Grub Street, ceased to be savant, poet, novelist, historian, philosopher, or amateur of books, to be all or none of these. He became precisely a writer who formed public opinion. Let me put it another way: it is as if the era of the book ended and the era of writing began. In any case, the writer in a sense replaced the saint: he became exemplary; he was looked upon for spiritual guidance. In the case of Rousseau, one may think of the cynics of Greece in opposition to the men and society of their time. Like Crates of Thebes, Rousseau gave up the signs of wealth, and therefore the values of society, to live according to an inner conviction of the truth. "It is something," he wrote Malesherbes, "to give men the example of the life they ought to live" (*Oeuvres complètes,* 1:1143). This attitude made him look with contempt upon the *gent littéraire.* "I think the peasants of Montmorency are more useful members of society than that heap of idle fellows paid with the fat of the people to chat in some academy six days a week; and I am more glad to do some good for my poor neighbors than help that crowd of petty intriguers which fills Paris succeed in their aspiration to be titled rascals" (p. 1143). Much the same thought is expressed in the discourse on the arts and sciences which made him famous in the first place, a work which is a denial of the values of the Republic of Letters as well as of the Temple of Fame.

But his discontent with letters had other implications. In his *Discours sur les richesses,* he deplores that men of letters should have become the supporters of men of wealth. Rousseau thought his fellow writers "cowardly adulators of wealth, even more cowardly detractors of poverty, who must prudently know how to accommodate their philosophy to the taste of those who pay for it" (quoted in Mario Einaudi, *The Early Rousseau,* p. 229). It is a view amply verified by Yves Durand in *Les Fermiers-généraux au dix-huitième siècle* (Paris, 1971), and J. P. Belin has also established a link between "philosophy" and the market. Rousseau, in other words, perceived what Julien Benda would later call a "trahison des clercs." Benda thought this treason occurred in the nineteenth century with nationalism, but it may be one could also find a treasonous betrayal of moral values to wealth in the second half of the eighteenth century, though again one would have to say the writers came out the losers. What seems to have happened is that the writers lined up with the new money, but this alignment was disguised by "philosophy" as universalizing discourse. They took a stand against fanaticism in the name of progress, reason, tolerance, and nature. In fact, their position worked against the remnants of feudal monarchy, already seriously altered by monarchical centralism and the impoverished nobility. The writers undoubtedly believed they (and the rich) did stand for civilization and enlightenment, an argument more valid then than now. The culture of the rich, evident in splendid collections and their patronage of letters and music, justified the new money power as arms in former times justified feudal power. Diderot's position in *Le Neveu de Rameau* is an excellent example of the universalizing aspect of language as expressed by Diderot-Moi: noble ideals are opposed to the concrete realities of gold, riches, and the misery of poverty. The issue is fought on the moral plane, with the help of noble abstractions such as humanity, justice, beauty, and truth. But like Liza Doolittle's father, the nephew could not afford morality, and perhaps this association of poverty with vice may have seemed to a man like Rousseau to be a rich man's argument. If one accepts Donal O'Gorman's analysis in *Diderot the Satirist,* then one may say that Diderot, the successful, established editor of the *Encyclopédie,* a capitalist enterprise, refutes the unsuccessful musician Rousseau. The nephew dares to sing to gold; Diderot does not; he sings of virtue and utility, but from the comfort of an established position, even though he was not rich. But to Rousseau, he seemed on the side of the rich. Rousseau's gesture of independence was a class as well as moral gesture. He meant to stay poor and independent rather than not be himself. Therefore it was also the gesture of the man of letters in the new literary space of the expanded marketplace. To escape the market one must above all not make of writing a métier.

This antiprofessional view is further developed in the first dialogue of *Rousseau juge de Jean-Jacques.* There he speaks of literature in connection with the ideal state of man, which is the state of nature, not in historical time, but in some ideal construction of the mind. In this ideal state few books are written, for to write is not a métier. Indeed, in this ideal world only one type of book exists, the one that *had* to be written, an imperative to truth which acts as a far stronger spur than the glory of the Temple of Fame. And in that state, once something has been written or said, the writer falls silent.

> When everyone will have said what he had to say, he will remain silent as before, without getting involved in literary gambling, without feeling that radical itch to twaddle and eternally smear paper which are said to be inseparable from the writer's trade; and one such perhaps, born with genius, will never even suspect it of himself, and die unknown to anyone if nothing arises to animate his zeal to the point of forcing him to show himself.

[P. 673]

Rousseau, like Blanchot in the twentieth century, though in different terms, envisaged the possible end of literature, for after all a great deal of literature thrives on what it is not necessary to say. Rousseau's language is extremely contemptuous—"literary gambling" (*tripot littéraire*), "itch to twaddle" (*démangeaison de rabâcher*), "smear paper" (*barbouiller*)—and sums up well enough the Grub Street aspect of literary production at the time. He posits a world without literature which, along with the other arts, is merely an aspect of the fall from grace, the fall from nature into society, or to use his images, from silence into twaddle. And the *tripot littéraire* is as inevitable in the state of society as sin after the Fall; literature could thus be considered, among other things, as the experience of man after the Fall. In his ideal world one writes from inner conviction, a position which makes possible the discovery of the counterfeiters of literature. The distinction between the unsuccessful hack and the successful established writer is once more modified. There are hacks, more or less successful, more or less rich, and there are those who have something to say. For Rousseau the writer writes not *with* society, but in spite of it, or even against it. In Rousseau's imagination such an experience was in sharp contrast with the world of music, for in the first part of this strange work of self-analysis, he associates music with happiness and the literary Jean-Jacques with misfortune.

In the same work, Rousseau also discusses his written works and his public image; that is, he deals with the difference between true self and appearance. He supposes thereby a new beyond; it is neither the perfection poets sought to attain as they polished their works even on Parnassus nor the theological beyond. The new beyond is that interior space already alluded to; it was the last refuge of the man of letters in a society which held him in contempt. Despite his poverty, he escaped in imagination. But Rousseau does something far more interesting with this inner dimension: he separates the author from the man. In earlier criticism this had not been the case. Critics did posit an objective literary standard of excellence, but they also hardly ever failed to turn a writer's words against him. Positing the author as an *other,* as Rousseau does in *Rousseau juge de Jean-Jacques,* makes possible another literary space, one free of personalities, above history, and beyond the market. Rousseau found thinking difficult; he did not like to write; he did not like correcting manuscripts or writing methodical books; and so thinking and writing for a living seemed to him a ridiculous occupation. Earning money by copying music meant that he merely sold the work of his hands. "The productions of my soul are not for sale; their disinterestedness alone can give them force and elevation" (p. 839). Rousseau's position is novel, for he separates not only author from man and author from society, but also author from riches. His poverty is raised to the level of nobility of soul, and the treason of the intellectuals he points to implicitly consists in selling out to the monied elite. "I have written books, true, but I never was a book scribbler [*livrier*]" (p. 840). Besides, to write is to put oneself at the public's mercy. "It would have been a question not of teaching and correcting, but of pleasing and succeeding" (p. 841). It is an interesting variation on the aesthetic cliché that the writer must please and instruct; here the emphasis no longer is on pleasing and succeeding in society. Rousseau assumed that by 1770 the public itself was no longer independent, but was being led by the nose by the hypocritical philosophical party which preached virtue while its metaphysical materialistic system, as witness d'Holbach, rendered virtue impossible. Nonetheless, virtue was dangled before the public as a necessary amusement for the people.

There is something modern about Rousseau, not only in his romanticism and alienation, but in his experience of literature which is continuous with his experience of society and of the self. Like Voltaire, he became a literary success, a celebrity and an international figure. But what is more striking is that he achieved this outside the bounds prescribed for such success at the time, outside the academies and other institutions which integrated the writer into society. More important, he was a writer who thought about the act of writing when few if any did so and who, like Linguet, thought of literature in negative terms. Yet although he thought of writing as an alienating activity, he was wrong to blame literature for his fall, for he found what he was through it and the paradox of success. If Voltaire in a sense changed the face of literature through his very facility, literature changed Rousseau, created him, made of him a writer *malgré lui*.

He also found that writing was an action the consequences of which had escaped Baillet's analysis. Rousseau saw his success as his perdition, and it may well have prompted the question, "What have I done?" Writing a book had ceased to be a matter of scholarship or art; instead it was a form of action in the moral sphere. Yet by separating the author from the man, Rousseau from Jean-Jacques, an autonomous literary space had been created. After Rousseau, the writer stood in a literary space which no longer belonged to the constructions of the Old Régime. It was with good reason Rousseau was never even a candidate to the Académie française.

## The Visible Temple

Fréron thought that by 1773 the philosophes had revolutionized literature and captured all the approaches to Parnasus. He was quite right: they had gained an impregnable foothold within the visible Temple of Fame, the Académie française which was to the metaphor of the Temple of Fame what the real visible church was to the eternal invisible church. But though Fréron may have deplored the philosophic party's position, it must be said that its victory was also a victory for men of letters in general. Fréron accurately saw it as a partisan victory, but in historical retrospect it can also be construed as something more. Two men were highly important in this development—Duclos and d'Alembert. But to understand their role and importance for the position of letters within the new literary space of the marketplace, it is necessary to look briefly at the history of the Académie française in the eighteenth century.

Founded by Richelieu ostensibly to fix the language but also as a means of political control of opinion, the Académie française had by the eighteenth century become a state ornament, dominated by bishops and great lords, with a minority of men of letters. It was mocked by Voltaire in the *Lettres philosophiques,* by Montesquieu in the *Lettres persanes,* by Desfontaines and Fréron, and it was the object of Piron's wit on several occasions:

> In France, by a pleasant means
> An author's shut off when to death he bores;
> In the Academy's fortieth seat he is put,
> Where gently he dozes and naught does but sleep;
> This chair is thus to wit
> As the conjugal bed is to love.

Or there is his deservedly famous epitaph to himself:

> Here lies Piron who nothing was,
> Not even of the Academy.

Even the abbé d'Olivet, one of the few men of letters who was a member in the early eighteenth century, and very much an academic type, thought its choice of members hardly inspired. It was an institution dominated by conformity, traditionalism, self-conceit, and the cult of Louis XIV. As Voltaire put it in an epistle to the regent:

> Upon his throne did Louis Flattery invite,
> And as an idol was incensed;
> Of eulogies Parnassus at last exhausted,
> Pious thoughts in near-worn tones repeats,
> And with incense in hand the learn'd Academy
> By its monotony
> For fifty years did make him sleep.

Few were the men of talents admitted to it: Dubos, d'Olivet, Alary, and Foncemagne. Yet the duc de Richelieu was admitted at the age of twenty-four, and the bishop of Bussy-Rabutin, the duc de Coislin, and the bishop of Luynes, none of whom were men of letters, were members. Others were the duc de Saint-Aignan, the duc de La Trémoille, the maréchal de Villars, d'Estrées, Amelot, the abbé de La Ville, and the abbé de Saint-Cyr, subpreceptor to the dauphin. Some women played influential roles in elections: Madame de Lambert used what influence she had to get Montesquieu elected in 1725, but his election was not ratified because he did not reside in Paris. Reelected in 1727, his victory was vetoed by Cardinal Fleury, and it was not until 1728 that he was finally received into the august company of the forty immortals. Louis Racine, a poet of considerable accomplishment and far more interesting than modern literary manuals would have it, was kept out for the Jansenist tendencies in his poem "La Grâce." Boyer, bishop of Mirepoix and Fleury, also kept out the well-known historian Charles Rollin, and even the abbé de La Bletterie was refused for having believed in the miracles of Deacon Pâris of the *convulsionnaire* fame. In 1733, Paradis de Moncrif, author of the *Histoire des chats,* was elected thanks to the influence of the duc d'Orleans. Marivaux, backed by LaMotte-Houdard, Fontenelle, and Madame de Tencin, had to wait ten years and was finally admitted after three attempts, in 1732, 1736, and 1742. Voltaire also had to try three times, to be finally received in 1746 after being blessed by Benedict XIV and flattering the Jesuits by remarks on Pascal's thoughts and a refutation of his *Provinciales.* Social respectability, rank, and religious conformity played a more important part in elections than did literary value.

Madame de Rochefort and Madame de Forcalquier intrigued to get Duclos elected to the Academy, even though he produced very little indeed, but at least he knew exactly what he wanted and what the Academy ought to be. He knew that it could be used to create a solid group of distinguished men of letters and amateurs of literature under the protection and patronage of the king, thereby stimulating talent among writers and cultivating the literary taste of town and court. Letters would be accorded greater respect, and the Academy could become the representative of the best and highest talent in the nation. Duclos fought against the practice of appointing members simply because they had been named for seats in high places, and when a protegé of Bishop Boyer was proposed for membership and the candidate alleged his shaky health as an argument for immediate election, Duclos replied with a famous bon mot: "The Academy has not been created to administer extreme unction." He knew it was meant as the institution for the best talents in letters, and he was instrumental in getting Buffon elected, and later d'Alembert.

The year 1760 was an important one in the history of the Academy, because it was then Lefranc de Pompignan, a protegé of the queen, Marie Leczinska, was elected and turned his reception speech into a general attack on the philosophes. They began to realize the importance of possessing seats in an institution which had regained its prestige, but which was also more and more divided into the two rival factions of the *parti dévot* and the *parti philosophique*. Vacant seats were thus contested along party lines until the election of d'Alembert to the secretaryship in 1773. With this election the success of the philosophic party was assured, and Fréron is proven to have been right. But what the famous critic did not say was that this triumph also meant the complete reestablishment of the Academy's reputation. Under d'Alembert's secretaryship it enjoyed international respect: discourses, receptions, and public sessions were important events, and the Academy was veritably the intellectual center of the nation. Fréron was also right in another respect, though he did not explicitly formulate his perception because it developed over a period of years and was inextricably connected with his personal fights with Voltaire and other philosophes: the philosophic party had become the literary establishment of the Old Régime on the eve of its demise. The implications of this are interesting because they offer a view of the writer which is an alternative to those of Rousseau and Diderot, a view which was expounded by d'Alembert and in a sense came to be realized in the Academy.

*163*

What may be called d'Alembert's concept of the man of letters is the result of his desire to maintain his independence within a system of patronage from on high; his solution differs from that of Rousseau, for whom the writer is a species of prophet; and it also differs from the example of Diderot, who was willing to work within the limits of literature as an aspect of capitalist investment and production in the name of enlightenment, humanity, and culture. D'Alembert's solution is par excellence that of the Old Régime, and though academies were abolished early in the Revolution, they were reestablished, and his idea survived well into the new régime and may still be firmly entrenched in the France of today.

D'Alembert set forth his views in three essays: the "Essai sur la société des gens de lettres et des grands" (1753); an unpublished essay of 1760 entitled "Réflexions sur l'état présent de la république des lettres"; and in the preface to his *Eloges lus dans les séances publiques de l'Académie française* (published in 1779, but read as a discourse in 1772). The problem is exposed in the first essay, which concerns the relation of the man of letters to the nobility, and d'Alembert shows a healthy suspicion of close links. There are certain advantages, to be sure. One is flattered, and wits ought to frequent society because it is a rich source for their writings, but it is best for those whose work requires study and meditation to avoid the whirl of the world. He also suspects that men of the world are not great judges of letters; the relation of men of letters to the great is all too often based on vanity, flattery, and ultimately dependence. The great danger lies here, for d'Alembert is intent on the need for independence and a professional attitude towards letters. He thinks that the only proper judges of a work are one's fellow professionals and colleagues. The implication is that men of letters were freeing themselves from the judgment of taste which was for so long attributed to *les honnêtes gens*. This philosophical view is based upon a certain historical perspective on the role of letters in their broad sense in society and history. Thus what made England great was precisely its men of letters, who taught the French the advantage of thinking freely. "Inferior to the French nation in matters of taste and pleasure, but of superior merit, at least by the great number of excellent philosophers it has produced, it has little by little communicated to us through its writings that precious liberty of thought from which reason profits, which a few wits abuse, and which fools disapprove" (*Oeuvres,* 4:351). Thus the writer or scholar need not feel any sense of inferiority towards the great, but he must take heed of the price to be paid for liberty. According to d'Alembert, his device ought to be: "LIBERTY, TRUTH, AND POVERTY (for if you fear the last, you are far from the other two), are three words which men of letters ought to ever have before them, as sovereigns that of POSTERITY" (4:367–68). The allusion to sovereigns is an appeal to patronage from the Crown, for if d'Alembert is suspicious of the great of this world, he thinks of the monarchy in different terms altogether. Because the sovereign can only benefit from enlightenment, it is to his advantage to protect and encourage letters, as did Charles V, Francis I, and Louis XIV.

By 1760 the same argument is still used, but more forcefully. D'Alembert by then was pensioned by Frederick the Great as well as Louis XV, thanks to his own talents and not to flattery of the great. As an Academician he posed the idea of the philosophe as a strong, virtuous, noble soul, equal to the great, owing nothing to anyone, and independent if poor. Elected perpetual secretary of the Academy in 1772, d'Alembert, now head of an institution composed of the great as well as men of letters, tried to conciliate them with the great. His success was made possible by the very nature of the Academy, in which all were, as Duclos had already made the point, equal. And so in the preface to his eulogies he also defined the philosophe as Academician, and thereby offered an image of the man of letters which was novel in its emphasis on the integration of the man of letters into a respectable body. "He who marries, says Bacon, gives hostages to Fortune; the man of letters who aspires to the Academy gives hostages to decency. This chain, all the more strong in that it is voluntary, will keep him without effort within limits he might otherwise have been tempted to cross. The isolated writer who wishes to remain so is a species of bachelor who, having less to be careful about, is thereby more subject or exposed to deviations" (*Eloges,* p. xvi). Within the context of the times, the implication seems to be that if Rousseau had been a member of the Academy he would have behaved decently. In short, being a member of the Academy insured the writer's respectability, and it was only within it that the poet and the pedant could lose those traits which rendered them unacceptable to and in society. The problem of the man of letters has thus been transcended by the creation of an elite.

The philosophe was not an ordinary writer, nor a scholar, nor a poet, nor a dramatist; he might be all of these or any one of them, but he was also something more. He was the representative of *les lumières,* of the light which had brought truth and reason to mankind after centuries of darkness, and as such he considered himself a leader of mankind. It was an elitist view of the thinker's task and does not at all imply democracy, nor even life, liberty, and the pursuit of happiness. It is a view which would become that of the notables of the new régime and could also be associated with enlightened despotism. According to this notion of the role of the man of letters, the individual writer's life must be exemplary and beyond reproach. As d'Alembert put it in a letter to Voltaire: "I act like Horace. I wrap myself up in my virtue; I neither fear nor expect anything from anybody; my behavior and my writings speak for me to those who care to listen to them. I defy calumny to do its worst" (quoted in Ronald Grimsley, *Jean d'Alembert,* p. 121). The allusion to antiquity is of interest: the ancient image of the sage is rejuvenated and turned into a citizen, and the philosophe is no longer the metaphysician of old who had his place within the literary space of the library. But despite all d'Alembert says and writes in favor of study and reflection, and despite his suspicion of salons, the image of the philosophe he and his fellow encyclopedists present supposes a space in which the antique sage is, after all, not alone. Though the public is looked upon with some reserve, though d'Alembert says, let the public pay heed if it will, he is aware of the existence of that public which, given the circumstances, is no longer the readership of the Republic of Letters. The philosophe supposes a space which is a forum for the ideas he has to propose, and at the same time, because he proposes ideas of universal validity, he must necessarily assume a moral and intellectual position in relation to humanity—and more precisely, the people, the murmuring fools he alludes to in his *Essai* of 1753, the fools afraid of the light of reason. D'Alembert thus poses a new type of aristocracy based on talent and through that talent equal to the nobility of the Old Régime.

Much the same view is proposed in *Le Neveu de Rameau,* a work in which Diderot-Moi is an image not only of Diderot but also of the philosophe. Since the book was intended to be a satire there is no doubt as to who is right and who is wrong, as there is no question on which side moral superiority lies. But the philosophes' fight was not an assault on Parnassus; Fréron's view of this was limited and too much informed by the established literary values of his youth. By the time the philosophes triumphed and controlled the avenues to Parnassus, the Temple of Fame was no longer believed in in quite the same way. Fame may still have been the spur for many men of letters and philosophes, but one suspects power was another, and certainly the fame they envisaged was not confined to literature and its perfection. In this the philosophes were at one with their opponent Rousseau, who as a prophet also meant to say something to that new entity, the public. The philosophic struggle implied more than literary questions because it involved writing in a general view of human destiny. Parnassus belonged to fable, but the philosophic struggle belonged to history. The result of this view of themselves which the philosophes espoused and successfully expounded must necessarily be a new approach to literary history, but like Moses, they were not destined to see that promised land in which they wanted to figure as the torchbearers of humanity. This work would be done by another generation, that of Barante and of Madame de Staël, while La Harpe, de Maistre, and de Bonald would perceive the same trend, but from an opposing point of view.

If one looks back upon the consciousness men of letters had of themselves and literature in the seventeenth century and well into the eighteenth, one does not find literary history written in terms of a progress. What one does find is a library—that is to say, a literary history or consciousness in terms of accumulated knowledge broad enough to include branches of knowledge from lyrical poetry to mathematics. The new literary history begins with the separation of the properly literary from the sciences. This was already realized by Father Goujet, whose literary history is broader than ours but less inclusive than Baillet's, and also more limited than Nicéron's biographical approach. But the decisive step was taken by d'Alembert in his "Preliminary Discourse" to the *Encyclopédie,* especially in the historical second part, in which the theory of the Renaissance is shifted in favor of philosophy. "When one considers the progress of the human mind since that memorable period [of the Renaissance], one finds these progresses were accomplished in the order they naturally had to follow. One began with erudition, continued through belles lettres, and finished by philosophy." The contiguity of disciplines which obtains in the literary space of the library is here replaced by succession in historical time, but a succession which is necessary as one moves from erudition to belles lettres to arrive at philosophy. Father Goujet's history of literature was still a *bibliothèque,* as he explained in his preface; he did not posit the superiority of one branch of knowledge over another. The literary space of the library was all-inclusive; d'Alembert's linear or developmental scheme is eliminatory. It tends to a greater and greater refinement of subject matter to arrive at a causality. This becomes evident in Prosper de Barante's *De la littérature française pendant le dix-huitième siècle* (1809), a work in which the relationship of eighteenth-century ideas to the Revolution are examined. Thus the opponents of the Revolution blame all of its ills on the philosophes.

> Isolating the eighteenth century from all the others, they look upon it as a cursed period in which an evil genius inspired writers with opinions which they spread among the people.

One would say, listening to them, that without the books of these writers everything would still be as in the seventeenth century; as if an age could transfer to its successor the heritage of the human mind as it received it from its predecessor.

[P. 3]

This is an excellent summary of the argument of the opponents of the Revolution, and one readily sees a certain conformity with the aesthetic of the eighteenth-century critics who measured the literary production of the time against the classical models of the age of Louis XIV. But, continues Barante, this fixity is impossible, and he thereby provides for a new reading of literary history. "Opinions have a necessary march. . . . That is what is called the march of civilization" (p. 4). In other words, something extraliterary, beyond the temple, beyond the library, has been posited as acting upon literature: the spirit of the times, or opinion, or the march of civilization, or even destiny. "It seems in a sense that the human spirit submits to the empire of necessity; that it is irrevocably destined to take such and such a road, at such and such a time, to accomplish a prescribed revolution, as do the stars" (p. 5).

Given this premise, literature is the expression of society, and the eighteenth century is viewed as a vast drama whose end was inevitable because the course of action was necessarily what it was. Literature is thus no longer a cause, a moral cause which must be guarded against, as in the case of books which might influence the uncritical, representing immoral actions, or even operating as a catharsis. Rather, literature is an effect of that destiny which makes for movement in historical time. The result is a rather abstract type of literary history. Barante can summarize eighteenth-century literature and science in seven pages without once mentioning the name of an author. A literary history without authors becomes possible because it is one of pure spirit, just as later on in the century art historians created an art history of pure visibility in which the names of the artists become incidental. It is a history very different indeed from the old *bibliothèques,* for it is without authors, without dates, without titles, and without bibliographical references. It is literary history as the history of ideas raised to a highly refined level of purity; it is literary history in an abstract space, far above Parnassus, far above Grub Street, beyond the library; it is voices in the rarefied atmosphere occupied by the elite.

### Arrival, Success, and Acceptance

The eighteenth-century French writer had before him several roads among which to choose in order to make a career in letters. There was that which led to the foot of Parnassus on which stood the Temple of Fame. It was a road which especially attracted poets and dramatists, but viewed from our perspective in history, that road led to stagnation. The writer bent on reaching that temple suffered from the very idea of its existence, because it signified that perfection had already been attained in a time past. The eighteenth-century author had to accept the handicap of living in an age which could only be inferior to the age of Louis XIV; his age, to use the language of T. S. Eliot, could not be one of absolute classicism, but only relatively so. The writers who aimed for the temple failed to survive through the works which were to gain them entrance to it; Voltaire, the best example because he was the man most motivated to reach and become the legislator of Parnassus, did not survive through the *Henriade* or *Mérope,* but through *Candide* and other writings which had no space reserved within the temple's small and selected library. The temple was thus likely to be a hindrance to writers but a boon to critics, for it gave the latter a ground to stand on from which they could judge the productions of the age. In the end the temple rested on a misunderstanding of the classics as something static, fixed, and perfect, a literature which perhaps existed only in the mind of the writer as the idea of a perfection to be attained, but which had somehow been affixed to certain existing models. And so the writers who sought the way of the temple found themselves engaged in the task of Sisyphus, endlessly trying to climb the same hill, ever failing to attain the perfection associated with Racine, Molière, Corneille, La Fontaine, Boileau, and the others already well established on Parnassus. The critics would always be there to tell them they had failed to reach the top and would never be admitted to the temple. That road was in fact a selective, narrow path which led to a dead end for literature.

But the writer who was not particularly inclined to be a poet could also choose a far more modest route. Rather than dream of Parnassus, he could take the road to the metaphoric library whose space was necessarily far larger than that of the temple atop a peak. And within the library there were many forms of writing to choose. But the space of the library was also destined to suffer an eclipse in the course of the century. It did not die and it was not abandoned, but it lost its prestige as literature came to be more narrowly defined and as the world of scholars came to be obscured by the more colorful, worldly, and talkative type of writer who might be a man about town, a member of an academy, or an affluent journalist-critic. The bustle and noise of Grub Street, in other words, tended to be more attractive, despite the poverty to be found there, than the library, because one might always hope to make a fortune from Grub Street by producing a work which caught the public's fancy or was noticed at court. Grub Street was the most crowded space of the period: a writer usually began there, and proceeded either to the temple (but hardly to the library) or to the new area of philosophy, which created a literary space no longer associated with either the temple or the library, and was located above Grub Street, bordering on the social space of the monied class.

As Fréron shrewdly observed, the space of philosophy was that of a new literature which had been turned into a weapon for the creation of public opinion, into a machine against established institutions and authorities, and which sold. The literature of Parnassus had rested on aesthetic and moral foundations which derived from antique pagan as well as Christian moral values and long-established literary forms. Much of the literature of the space of the library was of scholarship and knowledge concerned with the ancient and Chris-

171

tian world as constituted and considered in terms of eternal verities. The literature of the Enlightenment was built on temporal values, directed to temporal ends, and brought temporal benefits. And if in the eighteenth century the temple could no longer be attained with any certainty because of the "burden of the past," the Académie française, on the other hand, could be reached and captured, as it was by the new literature. But philosophy also meant something else: the man of letters had at last become part of a social-intellectual elite, even though the old contempt was by no means gone. The Academy and the prestige it gave the man of letters was such that the profession as a whole stood to benefit, at least in self-esteem.

Thus the spaces I have described also contain different and appropriate portraits of the man of letters in the society of the Old Régime, and more particularly in the eighteenth century. The penniless poet and the ridiculous pedant were no longer common images. The library evokes a whole class of learned priests, obscure writers, and scholars, as well as the *lettrés* of the parlementary class, those directly connected with libraries, such as specialists in oriental languages and ancient manuscripts, and other men of books, such as bibliophiles and the directors of the many Parisian libraries. One thinks of the many painted and printed portraits of scholars and readers produced, for example, by Rembrandt.

The space of Parnassus calls for an entirely different imagery and portraiture. Besides the set imagery of Parnassus and the temple and Apollo presiding over an assembly of hierarchically arranged poets and painters, one may also imagine the aspirant to the temple, while still in the sublunary world, as the young, handsome, ebullient, mercurial Voltaire, depicted by Jordan in his literary travels and painted by Largillière. Voltaire, the rival of Crébillon the elder, who crushed Lefranc but paid heed to Piron's wit, and who was ceaselessly at odds with the critics. It is an image, not of study and meditation in an interior space, of a man bent over quartos and folios, but of the *bel esprit* with ambition.

As for Grub Street, one must of course read the great literary portrait of it in *Le Neveu de Rameau,* evoke the cheva-

172

lier de La Morlière and his claque and the chevalier de Mouhy and his pen for hire, as well as a growing army of journalists and hacks working for the book factory of that great compiler of dictionaries, the abbé de La Porte.

Finally, the philosophe offers a different image. He is respectable, the man of letters integrated in society, seated in a salon, warming himself by the fire, at table with d'Holbach, or calling upon Voltaire. These are images by Carmontelle and Huber, far removed from the more austere space and portraiture of the grave readers of the library. Literature has turned to wit and conversation, the play and effect of ideas, correspondence with monarchs, and discourses in the Academy. The philosophe is accepted at last in some circles and is sure of his role in society and history. The portrait of Voltaire by Largillière yields to Houdon's seated Voltaire in the guise of an antique sage: the writer too is worthy of a monument.

# Selected Bibliography

## Primary sources

*Addition à l'ouvrage intitulé: Les Trois Siècles de notre littérature; ou, Lettre critique adressée à M. l'abbé Sabatier de Castres, soi-disant auteur de ce dictionnaire.* Amsterdam, 1773.

Alembert, Jean Le Rond d'. *Eloges lus dans les séances publiques de l'Académie française.* Paris, 1779.

————. *Mélanges de littérature, d'histoire, et de philosophie.* 5 vols. 4th ed. Amsterdam, 1767.

*Anecdotes secrètes pour servir à l'histoire de la république des lettres en France depuis 1762 jusqu'à nos jours.* 4 vols. London: Adamson, 1779–80.

Argens, Jean-Baptiste Boyer, Marquis d'. *Mémoires de M. le marquis d'Argens, avec quelques lettres sur divers sujets.* London, 1735.

————. *Mémoires secrets de la république des lettres; ou, Le Théâtre de la vérité.* 6 vols. Amsterdam, 1737–40.

[Aublet de Maubuy?] *Histoire des troubles et démêlés littéraires depuis leur origine jusqu'à nos jours inclusivement.* Amsterdam and Paris, 1779.

Baillet, Adrien. *Jugements des savants sur les principaux ouvrages des auteurs . . . revus, corrigés, et augmentés par M. de La Monnoye.* 7 vols. Paris, 1722–30.

Barante, Prosper de. *De la littérature française pendant le dix-huitième siècle.* Paris: L. Colin, 1809.

Bartoli, Daniello. *L'Homme de lettres.* Translated by Father Timothée de Livoy. Paris, 1768.

Basnage, Henri. *Histoire des ouvrages des savants.* 25 vols. Rotterdam, 1687–1709.

Beffroy de Reigny, Louis Abel [Cousin Jacques]. *Les Petites Maisons du Parnasse: Ouvrage comico-littéraire d'un genre nouveau, en vers et en prose.* Bouillon, 1783–84.

Bruys, François. *Critique désinteressée des journeaux littéraires et des ouvrages des savants.* 3 vols. The Hague, 1730.

Bruzen de La Martinière, Antoine Augustin. *Introduction générale à l'étude des sciences et des belles lettres en faveur des personnes qui ne savent que le français.* The Hague, 1731.

Chaudon, Dom Louis Mayeul. *Bibliothèque d'un homme de goût; ou, Avis sur le choix des meilleurs livres écrits en notre langue sur tous les genres de science et de littérature.* 2 vols. Avignon, 1772.

Deleyre, Alexandre. *Le Revue des feuilles de M. Fr.* London, 1756.

Delisle de Sales, Jean-B.-Claude Izouard. *Essai sur le journalisme depuis 1735 jusqu'à 1800.* Paris, 1811.

Denina, Carlo. *Tableau des révolutions de la littérature ancienne et moderne.* Paris, 1767.

Desfontaines, Pierre François Guyot. *Le Nouvelliste du Parnasse; ou, Réflexions sur les ouvrages nouveaux.* 2 vols. Paris, 1734.

———. *Paradoxes littéraires au sujet de la tragedie "d'Inès de Castro."* Paris, 1723.

———. *Voltairomanie; ou Lettre d'un jeune avocat, en forme de mémoire en réponse au libelle du sieur de Voltaire intitulé "Le Préservatif."* Paris, 1738.

Diderot, Denis. *Sur la liberté de la presse.* Edited by Jacques Proust. Paris: Editions sociales, 1964.

Dixmérie, Bricaire de La, Nicolas. *Les Deux Ages du goût et du génie français sous Louis XIV et sous Louis XV.* Paris, 1770.

Doigny du Ponceau. *La Dignité des gens de lettres: Pièce qui a concouru pour le prix de l'Académie française en 1774.* Paris, 1774.

———. *Epître à un homme de lettres célibataire.* Paris, 1773.

Duclos, Charles Pinot. *Considérations sur les moeurs de ce siècle.* 6th ed. Paris, 1772.

Fenouillot de Falbaire, Georges. *Avis aux gens de lettres.* Liège, 1770.

Formey, Jean-Henri-Samuel. *Conseils pour former une bibliothèque peu nombreuse mais choisie.* Berlin, 1757.

———. *La France littéraire; ou, Dictionnaire des auteurs vivants.* Berlin, 1757.

Fougeret de Monbron, Louis Charles. *Le Cosmopolite; ou, Le Citoyen du monde.* London, 1753.

Fréron, Elie Catherine. *L'Année littéraire.* 198 vols. Paris, 1754–75.

———. *Les Confessions de Fréron (1719–1776): Sa vie, souvenirs intîmes et anecdotes, ses pensées.* Edited by Charles Barthelemy. Paris: Charpentier, 1876.

————. *Lettres de Madame la comtesse de* ———— *sur quelques écrits de ce temps.* 13 vols. Paris, 1749–54.

————. *Opuscules.* 3 vols. Amsterdam, 1753.

Garat, Dominique-Joseph. *Mémoires historiques sur la vie de M. Suard, sur ses écrits, et sur le dix-huitième siècle.* Paris, 1820.

Garnier, Jean-Jacques. *L'Homme de lettres.* Paris, 1764.

Gédoyn, Nicolas. *Recueil d'opuscules littéraires.* Amsterdam, 1767.

Goujet, Claude Pierre. *Bibliothèque française; ou, Histoire de la littérature française.* 18 vols. Paris, 1740–56.

————. *Mémoires historiques et littéraires.* The Hague, 1767.

Huet, Daniel. *Huetiana; ou Pensées diverses de M. Huet, évêque d'Avranches.* Paris, 1722.

Irailh, Simon Augustin. *Querelles littéraires; ou, Mémoires pour servir à l'histoire des révolutions de la république des lettres.* 4 vols. Paris, 1761.

Jordan, Charles-Etienne. *Histoire d'un voyage littéraire fait en 1733 en France, Angleterre, et Hollande.* The Hague, 1735.

————. *Recueil de littérature, de philosophie, et d'histoire,* Amsterdam, 1730.

Juvenel de Carlencas, Félix de. *Essais sur l'histoire des belles lettres, des sciences, et des arts.* 4 vols. Paris, 1749.

La Harpe, Jean-François. *Letters to the Shuvalovs.* Edited by Christopher Todd. Studies on Voltaire and the Eighteenth Century, vol. 108. Banbury, England, 1973.

————. *Lycée; ou, Cours de littérature ancienne et moderne.* 16 vols. Paris, 1815.

————. *Mélanges littéraires; ou, Epîtres et pièces philosophiques.* Paris, 1765.

Lambert, Claude-François. *Histoire littéraire du règne de Louis XIV.* 3 vols. Paris, 1751.

La Monnoye, Bernard de. *Oeuvres choisies.* 3 vols. Dijon, 1769–70.

Landine, Antoine-François de. *Couronnes académiques; ou, Recueil des prix.* Paris, 1787.

Lefèvre, Antoine-Martial. *Les Muses en France.* Paris, 1750.

Marivaux, Pierre Carlet de Chamblain de. *Le Cabinet du philosophe.* Paris, 1734.

————. *L'Indigent philosophe.* Paris, 1728.

Marmontel, Jean-François. *Mémoires.* In *Oeuvres complètes,* vols. 1, 2. Paris, 1818–20.

Ménage, Gilles. *Anti-Baillet; ou, Critique du livre de M. Baillet.* Paris, 1730.

Mercier, Louis-Sébastien. *Les Entretiens du Palais Royal.* Paris, 1786.

————. *De la littérature et des littérateurs.* Yverdon, 1778.

———— *Du bonheur des gens de lettres.* London and Paris, 1766.

Meunier de Querlon, Anne-Gabriel. *Lettre d'un avocat de Rouen à M. V——— au sujet de feu abbé Desfontaines.* Paris, 1746.

Morellet, André. *Mémoires inédits . . . sur le dix-huitième siècle et sur la Révolution.* 2d ed. 2 vols. Paris, 1822.

Moréri, Louis. *Le Grand Dictionnaire historique; ou, Mélange curieux de l'histoire sacrée et profane.* 10 vols. Paris, 1759.

Morlière, Charles-Jacques-Louis-Auguste Rochette de La. *Angola, histoire indienne.* Paris, 1746.

————. *Le Contre-poison des feuilles.* Paris, [1754].

Mouhy, Charles le Pieux, Chevalier de. *Le Mérite vengé; ou, Conversations littéraires et variées sur divers écrits modernes, pour servir de réponse aux observations de l'ADF.* Amsterdam, 1737.

Nicéron, Jean-Pierre. *Mémoires pour servir à l'histoire des hommes illustres dans la république des lettres.* 43 vols. Paris, 1727–45.

*Observations pour servir á l'histoire des gens de lettres qui ont vécu dans ce siècle-ci.* Paris, 1751.

Palissot, Charles. *Apollon mentor; ou, Le Télémaque moderne.* London, 1748.

————. *Oeuvres.* 4 vols. Paris, 1788.

Pérau, Gabriel Louis Calabre. *Vie de Jerôme Bignon, avocat-général et conseiller d'état.* Paris, 1757.

Pidansat de Mairobert. *L'Espion anglais; ou, Correspondance secrète entre Milord All'eye et Milord All'ear.* New and rev. ed. 10 vols. London: Adamson, 1779.

Porte, Joseph de La. *L'Esprit de l'abbé Desfontaines; ou, Réflexions sur différents genres de science et de littérature avec des jugements sur quelques auteurs et sur quelques ouvrages tant anciens que modernes.* 4 vols. London, 1757.

————. *Nouvelle bibliothèque d'un homme de goût; ou, Tableau de la littérature ancienne et moderne de Dom Chaudon.* New and rev. ed. 4 vols. Paris, 1777.

————. *Voyage en l'autre monde.* London, 1752.

Raynal, Guillaume-Thomas-François. *Anecdotes littéraires; ou, Histoire de ce qui est arrivé de plus singulier et de plus intéressant aux écrivains français depuis François Ier jusqu'à nos jours.* 2 vols. Paris, 1750.

Rigoley de Juvigny, Jean-Antoine. *De la décadence des lettres et des moeurs, depuis les Grecs et les Romains jusqu'à nos jours.* Paris, 1787.

Rivarol, Antoine, Comte de, and Champcenetz, Louis de. *Le Petit Almanach de nos grands hommes pour l'année 1788.* Paris, 1788.

Romagnesi, Jean-Antoine, and Niveaux. *Le Temple du goust.* Paris, 1733.

Rousseau, Jean-Jacques. *Confessions.* In *Oeuvres complètes,* vol. 1. Paris: Pléiade, 1959.

———. *Rousseau juge de Jean-Jacques.* In *Oeuvres complètes,* vol. 1. Paris: Pléiade, 1959.

Sabatier de Castres, Antoine. *Correspondance littéraire critique et secrète; ou, Supplément aux "Trois Siècles de la littérature française" de M. l'abbé S———.* London, 1782.

———. *Tableau philosophique de l'esprit de Monsieur de Voltaire pour servir de suite à ses ouvrages, et de mémoires à l'histoire de sa vie.* Geneva, 1771.

———. *Les Trois Siècles de la littérature française; ou, Tableau de l'esprit de nos écrivains depuis François Ier jusqu'en 1774, en forme de dictionnaire.* New and augmented ed. 4 vols. Amsterdam, 1775.

Saint-Hyacinthe, Thémiseuil de. *Le Chef d'oeuvre d'un inconnu, poème heureusement découvert et mis au jour, avec des remarques savantes et recherchées, par M. le docteur Chrisostome Mathanasius.* 6th ed. 2 vols. The Hague, 1732.

Saint-Sauveur, Rémond de. *Agenda des auteurs.* Paris, 1755.

Sallengre, Albert-Henri de. *Histoire de Pierre de Montmaur.* 2 vols. The Hague, 1715.

———. *Mémoires de littérature.* 3 vols. The Hague, 1715–17.

Saugrain, Claude Marin. *Code de la librairie et imprimerie de Paris.* Paris, 1744.

Suard, Jean-Baptiste-Antoine. *Discours impartial sur les affaires actuelles de la librairie.* N. p., 1777.

———. *Variétés littéraires.* 4 vols. Paris, 1768–69.

Tissot, Samuel A. A. D. *De la santé des gens de lettres.* Lausanne and Paris, 1768.

Titon Du Tillet, Evrard. *Description du Parnasse français.* Paris, 1727.

———. *Essais sur les honneurs et sur les monuments accordés aux illustres savants pendant la suite des siècles.* Paris, 1734.

Travenol, Louis, and Maunoury, Louis. *Voltairiana; ou, Eloges amphigouriques de Fr. Marie Arrouet, sieur de Voltaire.* Rev. ed. Paris, 1749.

Vigneul-Marville, Noël Argonne. *Mélanges d'histoire et de littérature.* 2 vols. Rouen, 1699–1700.

Voisenon, Claude-Henri de Fusée de. *Anecdotes littéraires.* Paris; Librairie des bibliophiles, 1880.

Voltaire, François Marie Arouet de. *Dictionnaire philosophique.* Edited by Julien Benda. Paris: Garnier 1954.

———. *Lettres choisies.* Edited by Raymond Naves. 2 vols. Paris: Garnier, 1946.

———. *Lettres philosophiques.* Edited by Raymond Naves. Paris: Garnier, 1962.

## Secondary sources

Albert-Buisson, François. *Les Quarante au temps des lumières.* Paris: Fayard, 1960.

Balcou, Jean. *Fréron contre les philosophes.* Geneva and Paris: Droz, 1975.

Bate, Walter Jackson. *The Burden of the Past and the English Poet.* New York: Norton, 1972.

Belin, Jean Paul, *Le Commerce des livres prohibés à Paris de 1750 à 1789.* Paris: Belin, 1913.

———. *Le Mouvement philosophique de 1748 à 1789.* Paris: Belin, 1913.

Besterman, Theodore. *Voltaire.* New York: Harcourt, Brace and World, 1969.

Birn, Raymond F. "Pierre Rousseau and the *Philosophes* of Bouillon." In *Studies on Voltaire and the Eighteenth Century,* vol. 29 (1964), pp. 11–203.

Blanchot, Maurice. *L'Espace littéraire.* Paris: Gallimard, 1968.

———. *Le Livre à venir.* Paris: Gallimard, 1971.

Boncompain, Jacques. *Auteurs et comédiens au XVIIIe siècle.* Paris: Librairie académique Perrin, 1976.

Brandes, Georg. *Voltaire.* 2 vols. Berlin: Erich Reiss Verlag, 1923.

Brengues, Jacques. *Charles Duclos (1704–1772); ou, L'Obsession de la vertu.* Saint-Brieuc: Presses universitaires de Bretagne, 1971.

———. "Duclos et Fréron frères ennemis." *Dix-huitième siècle* 2 (1970): 197–208.

Buchanan, Michelle. "Marmontel: Un Auteur à succès du XVIIIe siècle." In *Studies on Voltaire and the Eighteenth Century,* vol. 55. (1967), pp. 321–32.

Burmeister, Brigitte. "Les Paradoxes de Linguet." *Dix-huitième siècle* 7 (1975): 147–56.

Cristin, Claude. *Aux Origines de l'histoire littéraire.* Grenoble: Presses universitaires de Grenoble, 1973.

Dabezies, André. "L'Erudition et l'humour: Le Père Bougeant (1690–1743)." *Dix-huitième siècle* 9 (1977): 259–71.

Darnton, Robert. "The High Enlightenment and the Low-Life Literature in Pre-Revolutionary France." *Past and Present* 51 (1971): 81–115.

Delafarge, Daniel. *La vie et l'oeuvre de Palissot.* Paris: Hachette, 1912.

Démoris, René. *La Roman à la première personne.* Paris: Armand Colin, 1976.

Einaudi, Mario. *The Early Rousseau.* Ithaca, N.Y.: Cornell University Press, 1971.

Estivals, Robert. *La Statistique bibliographique de la France sous la monarchie au XVIIIe siècle.* Paris: Mouton, 1965.

Freud, Hilde. "Les *Philosophes* de Palissot." In *Diderot Studies*, vol. 9 (1967), pp. 20–243.

Garagnon, Jean, "Les *Memoires de Trévous* et l'évènement, ou Jean-Jacques Rousseau vu par les jésuites." *Dix-huitième siècle* 8 (1976): 215–36.

Green, Frederick C. *Eighteenth Century France.* London and Toronto: J. M. Dent and Sons, 1928.

Grimsley, Ronald. *Jean d'Alembert.* Oxford: Clarendon Press, 1963.

————. *Jean-Jacques Rousseau: A Study in Self-Awareness.* Cardiff: University of Wales Press, 1961.

Grosclaude, Pierre. *Malesherbes: Témoin de son temps.* Paris: Fischbacher, [1960].

Johnston, Elise. *Le Marquis d'Argens, sa vie et ses oeuvres.* Paris: Champion, 1928.

Jovicevich, Alexandre. *Jean-François de La Harpe, adepte et rénégat des lumières.* South Orange, N.J.: Seton Hall University Press, 1973.

Kermode, Frank. *The Classic: Literary Images of Permanence and Change.* New York: Viking, 1975.

Le Bourgo, Léo. *Un Homme de lettres au XVIIIe siècle: Duclos.* Bordeaux: Gounouilhou, 1902.

Lough, John. "Le Breton, Mills, et Sellius." *Dix-huitième siècle* 1 (1969): 267–87.

————. "Luneau de Boisjermain v. the Publishers of the *Encyclopédie*." In *Studies on Voltaire and the Eighteenth Century*, vol. 23 (1963), pp. 115–77.

Micard, Etienne. *Un Ecrivain académique au dix-huitième siècle: Thomas.* Paris: Champion, 1924.

Morris, Thelma. "L'Abbé Desfontaines et son rôle dans la littérature de son temps." In *Studies on Voltaire and the Eighteenth Century*, vol. 19 (1961), pp. 15–381.

Myers, Robert L. "Fréron's critique of Rémond de Saint-Mard." In *Studies on Voltaire and the Eighteenth Century*, vol. 37 (1965), pp. 147–64.

Neret, Jean-Alexis. *Histoire illustrée de la librairie et du livre français.* Paris: Lamarre, 1953.

Nisard, Charles. *Les Ennemis de Voltaire.* Paris: Amyot, 1853.

O'Gorman, Donal. *Diderot the Satirist.* Toronto: Toronto University Press, 1971.

Pappas, John. "Berthier's *Journal de Trévous* and the *Philosophes*." In *Studies on Voltaire and the Eighteenth Century*, vol. 3 (1957), pp. 9–233.

Pinkus, Philip. *Grub Street Stripped Bare.* London: Constable, 1968.

Proust, Jacques. *Diderot et l'Encyclopédie.* Paris: Colin, 1962.

Reed, Gervais E. *Claude Barbin: Libraire de Paris sous le règne de Louis XIV.* Geneva: Droz, 1974.

Rétat, Pierre. *"Mémoires pour l'histoire des sciences et des beaux-arts:* Signification d'un titre et d'une entreprise journalistique." *Dix-huitième siècle* 8 (1976): 167–88.

Roche, Daniel. "Un Savant et sa bibliothèque au XVIIIe siècle (Les Livres de Dortous de Mairan)." *Dix-huitième siècle* 1 (1969): 47–88.

Shaw, Edward P. "Censorship and Subterfuge in Eighteenth-century France." In *Literature and History in the Age of Ideas: Essays in Honor of George R. Havens,* edited by Charles G. S. Williams. Columbus: Ohio State University Press, 1975.

Spink, John Stephenson. "The Clandestine Book Trade in 1752: The Publication of the *Apologie de l'abbé de Prades."* In *Studies in Eighteenth Century French Literature Presented to Robert Niklaus.* Exeter: University of Exeter Press, 1975.

Todd, Christopher. *Voltaire's Disciple: Jean-François de La Harpe.* London: Modern Humanities Research Association, 1972.

Trenard, Louis. "La Presse périodique en Flandre au XVIIIe siècle." *Dix-huitième siècle* 1 (1969): 89–106; 2 (1970): 77–102.

Tucoo-Chala, Suzanne. "La Diffusion des lumières dans la seconde moitié du XVIIIe siècle: Ch. J. Panckoucke, Libraire éclairé (1760–1799)." *Dix-huitième siècle* 6 (1974): 115–28.

Wilson, Arthur M. *Diderot.* New York: Oxford University Press, 1972.

# INDEX

*183*

*185*

186

*Rémy G. Saisselin is professor of fine arts and professor of French literature at the University of Rochester. He has also taught at Western Reserve University and served as curator of publications at the Cleveland Museum of Art. Born in Switzerland, he received his B.A. from Queens College and M.A.s in French and history from the University of Wisconsin, where he also earned his Ph.D. in 1957. He has received both a Fulbright scholarship and a Guggenheim fellowship, and has been named correspondent réel at the Collège de Pataphysique. In addition to this book, Saisselin has published numerous articles and four previous books dealing with various aspects of French art and literature.*

*The manuscript was edited by Sherwyn T. Carr. The book was designed by Richard Kinney. The typeface for the text is Bembo, based on a copy of a roman cut by Francesco Griffo for the Venetian printer Aldus Manutius about 1495. The display face is Caslon Old Face with swash initials.*

*The text is printed on Lakewood Offset paper and the book is bound in Holliston's Kingston cloth over binder's boards.*

*Manufactured in the United States of America.*